DR. DROPO'S
JUGGLING BUFFOONERY

BY
BRUCE FIFE
A.K.A. DR. DROPO

JAVA PUBLISHING CO.
BELLAIRE, TEXAS

Copyright © 1988, Java Publishing Co.

ISBN 0-941599-05-1

TABLE OF CONTENTS

INTRODUCTION

Have you ever felt the excitement of watching a skilled comic juggler perform, and wish you could be as funny and as entertaining? As a novice juggler, I sure did.

When I first started to learn how to juggle, friends would beg me for a demonstration. Proudly I would attempt to satisfy their curiosity by doing the basic three ball cascade and one or two elementary tricks, showing them virtually everything I knew—but they wanted more. The few tricks I would do were nice, but I could see the anticipation in their faces for me to do or say something funny. A juggler to most people is a clown, and if you can juggle then you must be a funny person. Juggling and comedy fit together like a foot in a sock (or in my case like a foot in the mouth). My friends do think I'm the life of the party though—they must because they keep telling me I'm a fungi.

In my early attempts to demonstrate my juggling skill, I found that I didn't know any juggling jokes. I was at a loss, so I started to ad lib, saying and doing anything that popped into my head, which can be dangerous because some mighty weird stuff floats around up there. My jokes and movements seemed rather stupid to me, but to my surprise, my friends liked it!

I found that corney jokes combined with juggling can be hilariously funny. Gradually I added other bits and pieces of buffoonery and before

I knew it, I had developed enough material for an entire act. It took me several months of goofing around, and a respectable chunk of practice to develop the juggling skill I wanted in order to show a good variety of tricks and to arrange the jokes in a cohesive manner.

I didn't realize it until later, but as a beginner I had all the juggling skill I really needed to be a funny juggler. I've learned that juggling skill is not that important. A good juggling act does not require the performer to juggle five clubs, flaming torches, or chin saws. Sure, this type of juggling is interesting, but a good comedy act doesn't need fancy tricks. The more tricks you know, the greater variety you have to work with, but a relatively inexperienced juggler can design a good comedy act with only a few simple tricks.

Up until the time I gave my first staged performance, I had only seen one professional comedy juggler. Watching him was invaluable in giving me ideas for jokes and in helping me develop my own act, but it wasn't enough. At this time there were no books on how to be a funny juggler. I would have gladly given my award winning spit wad collection to have had a book like this one at the time; my wife would have been glad to see me give my prized collection away too—for any book. Without such a book, however, I was left on my own.

Since I didn't have a reference source to turn to, I relied on other jugglers. Although I copied some of their style, most the material I used was original. What I did borrow, I tried to changed to fit my own personality. In my opinion, in order to be a good comic juggler you need to develop your own material. Ideas and jokes can be copied, but you should change them enough to fit your own comic style.

From experience I've found that the hardest part in creating a funny routine is finding a starting point or theme. If you can find a suitable starting point, 90% of the battle is won. The rest will just follow.

The routines presented in this book are provided as examples of the type of comic juggling I do. They can provide you with some ideas and give you a starting point from which to create your own material.

This is not a joke book and is not meant to be read solely for entertainment; it is a workbook, designed to give you examples of

what can be done. Much of the humor expressed in these pages relies heavily on physical comedy. I have briefly described some of the the facial expressions and body movements I use, but as with any physical expression, you must act out the routines in order to fully appreciate the humor.

To get full benefit from this book, visualize each routine in your mind as if you were watching your favorite comedians. What type of mannerisms, facial expressions, and physical gestures would they use in the situations described? Keep this idea in mind while you read.

The book is divided into three sections. The first section begins with a simple description of how to juggle, using a method I have found successful as a juggling instructor. It also describes each juggling trick that is needed for the rest of the section, all of which are simple and easy to learn. Sixteen complete comic juggling routines follow. The second section introduces the art of balancing and explains how to balance objects like brooms and poles, followed by routines using these methods. The third section teaches how to manipulate cigar boxes, describes several simple tricks, and provides examples of comic cigar box routines.

Most of the routines described in this book require only elementary juggling skills. In fact, some of the routines contain no real juggling at all, relying solely on mime and comedy dialog. Even a nonjuggler can use them successfully. These routines are my favorites and have proven to be some of my most popular.

I have purposely reused as many juggling tricks as possible throughout the book so you won't get bogged down trying to learn new tricks for each routine. In many cases the type of trick used is of little importance. A beginner can read this book and learn how to juggle, do balancing tricks, manipulate cigar boxes, and create funny juggling routines. For those who already know how to juggle this book will provide a valuable source of creative ideas.

SECTION ONE:
JUGGLING

JUGGLING—THE EASY WAY

I will start this section off with a simple explanation of how to juggle—
the easy way. The system I use stresses a step-by-step progression,
beginning with one ball juggling and working up to three balls. For
readers who already know how to juggle three balls, you may want
to skip to the next heading entitled **Juggling Tricks**.

Step One

Before doing anything else, imagine two spots about forehead level,
one just to the right of your head and the other just to the left, see
Figure 1-1 on the next page. Both spots should be about a foot in
front of your face. These spots will be your control points and are
VERY IMPORTANT!

Take one ball into the palm of your right hand and hold it at about
stomach level. From the juggler's point of view it would look like
Figure 1-2. Toss the ball in the right hand across to the imaginary
spot on the left side of your forehead. When it comes down, catch
it in the left hand (Figure 1-3).

Figure 1-1

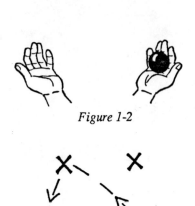

Figure 1-2

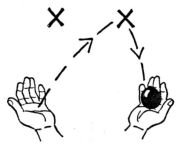

Figure 1-3

Toss the ball from your left hand up to the imaginary spot at the right side of your forehead. As it falls, catch it with your right hand (Figure 1-4). The ball has now made one round trip in a figure-eight pattern (Figure 1-5).

Practice this pattern with one ball, making sure it hits the imaginary spots on each side of your head. Don't throw the ball too hight or too low. Focus your attention at these spots and make your throws as consistent as possible.

As you practice, make sure not to reach up to grab the ball as it comes down. Let the ball fall into your hand. As you are learning make it a point never to raise you hands above chest level when either

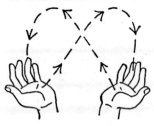

Figure 1-4

Figure 1-5

throwing or catching. Continue to practice this step until you feel comfortable with it.

Step Two

Now that you have mastered juggling one ball, you can try two. Put one ball in each hand. Keep your elbows bent, and your hands away from your body, but at stomach level.

Throw the ball in the right hand up to the imaginary spot on the left side of your head (Figure 1-6). When the ball reaches this spot, toss the ball which is in your left hand toward the imaginary spot on the right side of your head (Figure 1-7). As soon as you release the ball from your left hand, quickly catch, with your left hand, the ball thrown by the right hand. Finally, the right hand will catch the ball thrown by the left hand (Figure 1-8).

You have just made a simple two-ball exchange. The ball which started in the right hand, is now in the left and vice versa. Repeat this sequence, starting with the right hand until you can catch the balls every time.

It is important that the balls are thrown as close to the imaginary spots as possible. Don't watch

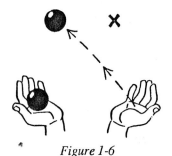

Figure 1-6

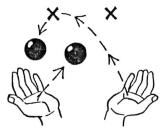

Figure 1-7

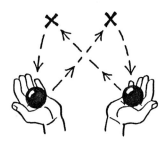

Figure 1-8

11

your hands or follow the movement of the balls; keep your eyes focused at the two imaginary points. I cannot emphasize this point enough. A ball that is not tossed correctly will throw off you timing, causing a drop. This will become more evident when you start to use three balls.

To help keep your timing consistent you might want to throw the balls as you say "right-left." Throw the ball in the right hand as you say "right." When it reaches the imaginary spot, say "left" and throw the left hand ball.

Step Three

Repeat the procedure in Step Two, except this time start by throwing the ball that is in the left hand first. This sounds easy, but at first it's a little more difficult than you might think. Continue to practice this step until you can catch the balls every time. When you can do this consistently, move on to Step Four.

Step Four

Take one ball in each hand. Imagine an invisible third ball in your right hand along with the real one already there. You now have one real ball in your left hand, and one real ball and one invisible ball in your right hand (Figure 1-9).

Begin by tossing the real ball from your right hand in the normal figure-eight pattern. Continue as you did in Step Two. When the first ball reaches the imaginary spot on the left side of your head, toss the second ball from your left hand toward the imaginary spot on the right (Figure 1-10). Quickly catch the first ball with the left hand.

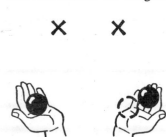

Figure 1-9

Up to this point you have been doing the same thing as you did in Step Two. But now here's the difference: as the second ball

12

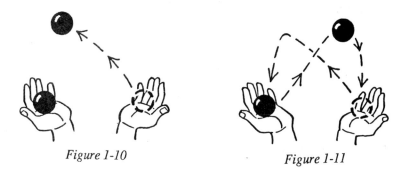

| Figure 1-10 | Figure 1-11 |

reaches the imaginary spot on the right, go through the motion of tossing the invisible third ball from the right hand before you catch the descending second ball (Figure 1-11).

This exercise gives you practice in throwing a third ball without the added worry of catching it. Practice until you feel confident with it.

Step Five

In this step you do the same thing as you did in Step Four, except this time replace the invisible ball with a real ball (Figure 1-12).

Proceed as you did in the last step. When you get to the point of throwing the third ball, concentrate on the accuracy of the throw. Make sure it goes to the imaginary spot on the left side of your head. Don't worry about catching it right now, let it drop to the floor.

The purpose of this step is to give you some practice in actually throwing the third ball and making the throw correctly. Check yourself as you practice this, making sure each of the three balls hit the imaginary spots.

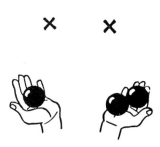

Figure 1-12

For some people this step will come easily and they will naturally move on to Step Six.

Step Six

Here it is, the final step. If you've practiced Steps One through Five and can perform them with confidence, this step will come much easier.

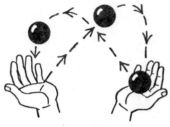

Figure 1-13

Pick up all three balls. Hold one ball in your left hand and two balls in your right. Do the same thing that you did in Step Five, but this time catch the third ball as it comes down. Make sure you throw the ball that is already in your hand before catching the next one.

Continue by tossing and catching each ball in succession. Don't Stop! Keep tossing the balls in the figure-eight pattern (Figure 1-13).

After the first two throws, the right hand is doing exactly the same thing as the left, catching and throwing the balls, that's all there is to it. If you can do this without stopping then you're juggling!

The jump between Steps Five and Six is a big one, and generally will require more practice than the other steps. Expect to spend some time on this. If you feel you're having more difficulty than you should, back up a step or two and practice that step some more. I guarantee that if you follow these steps and don't give up, you will learn to juggle.

JUGGLING TRICKS

The tricks described here are listed in alphabetical order and not by degree of difficulty. Most of the tricks necessary to perform the routines described later are contained here. Keep in mind, however, that there are many other tricks that will work in the routines just as well as those described here.

Behind the Back Toss

One ball is taken behind the juggler's back and tossed up over his shoulder. As it comes down it is caught and juggling continues.

Claw

The balls in this trick follow the same flight pattern as the cascade, only the way the balls are caught and thrown are different. Instead of catching the balls with the palms up, they are "clawed" downward. Claws can be done with one or both hands.

Columns

Instead of tossing the balls in a figure-eight pattern, as in the cascade, the balls are kept in vertical columns. The center ball is thrown straight up between the other two (Figure 1-14).

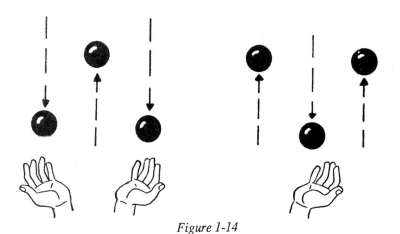

Figure 1-14

Elbow Bounce

One ball is bounced off the elbow as shown in Figure 1-15. The

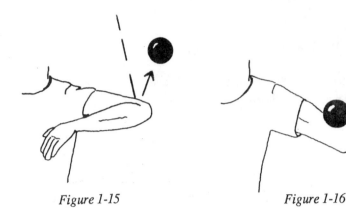

Figure 1-15   Figure 1-16

key to doing this trick correctly is to make contact with the ball while the elbow is in a horizontal position. If it is bent too far up or down, the ball will rebound sideways.

Elbow Catch

For this trick one of the balls is caught and held in the arm, between the biceps and forearm (Figure 1-16). From the cascade, reach up with your outstretched arm and catch one of the balls in the bend of you arm. Bend the arm quickly to prevent the ball from rolling off. From this position the ball can be snapped back up into the air and juggling resumed.

Ferris Wheel

The balls are thrown in a circular pattern as shown in Figure 1-17.

Figure 1-17

Floor Bounce

This is one of the all time easiest juggling   tricks to learn.   While juggling, toss one ball high up into the air and let it fall, bouncing on the ground.   As it rebounds on the bounce, catch it and continue juggling.

16

Foot Tap

When dropped on the floor a ball will rebound a foot or two. A light upward tap with the foot will give the ball enough of a boost upward so that it can be caught and juggled without stopping.

Forearm Bounce

The ball is bounced off the inside of the raised forearm (Figure 1-18). In order for the ball to bounce straight up, hit the ball when the arm is horizontal.

Figure 1-18

Knee Bounce

The ball is bounced off the top of the knee. The ball should hit just above the kneecap on the juggler's bent leg.

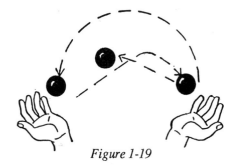

Over the Top

Two balls are juggled in the cascade pattern while the third is tossed in a high arc (Figure 1-19).

Figure 1-19

Shower

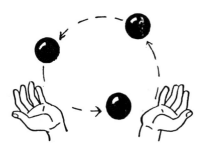

All the balls are thrown in a circular pattern as illustrated in Figure 1-20.

Figure 1-20

Short Floor Bounce

One ball is thrown downward onto the floor. As it bounces back up it is caught and juggling resumed.

Under the Arm Toss

One ball is caught and moved over and under the other arm before tossing it back up into the cascade. This trick can be done continuously under both arms using the same ball (Figure 1-21).

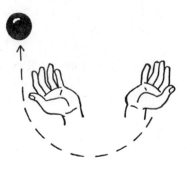

Figure 1-21

Under the Leg Toss

One ball is swung down and tossed up under the leg. This trick can be done with both legs alternately.

JUGGLING ROUTINES

EASY-KNEEZY-NOSEY

Props: Three balls, three juggling clubs, cowboy hat, shoe, football, cereal box, scarf, He-Man masters of the universe toy, and a baloney sandwich.

This is a relatively simple routine. An assistant is needed to help the juggler. Other than the balls and the clubs, the props can be varied. Juggler begins by doing the cascade with three balls.

"The juggling pattern you see me doing right now is the basic juggling pattern all jugglers perform. Any variations or deviations from this pattern are what's known as the juggler's tricks. For example, this movement is called the *under arm toss*. This next movement is called the *shower*." The juggler does each of these movements.

"For you farmers out there this one is called milking the goat." Juggler does *columns*.

Juggler does the *claw* with one hand. "This movement is called swatting flies at the picnic." Juggler does continuous three ball *claws*. "This is called standing next to a garbage truck."

Juggler begins jogging in place as he jugglers. "Here's one known as jogging in the park or the jogging juggler or simply the juggler."

"This next one is called the Richard Simmons juggle." Juggler lifts right leg then left counting in a high-pitched, Richard Simmons-type voice, "One and two and three and four. One and two and three . . . come on now let's get those legs up higher! Two and three and four."

Juggler now drops one ball on the floor. "That's called dropping the ball on the ground." As he bends down to pick it up he adds, "This is called picking the ball up off the ground. You would be surprised, but this is a very popular trick among jugglers. I have to do it every now and then just to keep in practice."

"This next trick is known as easy-kneezy-nosey." Juggler does the *knee bounce.* "It's called easy-kneezy-nosey because I have to hit the ball easy with my kneezy or it will bounce back up and hit me in my nosey."

"I will 1 now attempt the under the right leg toss." He does *under the leg toss.* "For those of you who missed it the first time here it is again. Now for those of you who are left handed here is the under the left leg toss." Juggler does both of these. "Now, for all those who thought I was just lucky, I will do both under the right leg and under the left leg toss at the same time." Juggler does continuous juggling under each leg.

He now repeatedly tosses one ball much higher than the other two as he cascades. "What's this?. . . It's a juggler with hiccups."

"I will now do the shoulder-arm-back-head bounce . . . ready?" One ball is batted with the juggler's forearm and sent rolling across the stage. "QUICK! Somebody grab that ball before it escapes . . . He's been trying to get out of this silly act for months."

"So far you have seen me do a lot of tricks with balls. I will now show you a breathless display of juggling with objects of different shape. First I will perform for you what is popularly known as the three-club juggle." Juggler pulls out three juggling clubs. "You are now about to see the famous three-club juggle." Performer starts to juggle but drops one before getting very far. He looks embarrassed and tries to think of an excuse. "Why . . . why . . . ah, that club must be defective or something. I can't juggle a defective club." He turns toward his assistant. "I need a replacement for this club, would you find one for me?"

The assistant looks in the prop bag and says, "We don't have any more clubs."

Juggler looks perplexed. "We don't? Hmm . . . well, let me use this instead." He grabs one of the balls. "Ladies and gentlemen, due to unforeseen circumstances I will have to substitute this ball for the defective club, so just pretend that this ball is just another club.

Now for the three-club juggle—" He starts to juggle but drops another club. "Why . . . It's . . . It's another defective club . . . I can't use that. Give me another substitute please." Assistant hands him a second ball. Juggler looks at the audience. "Ladies and gentlemen, just pretend that this is just another club. Now here we go." As he begins to juggle the two balls and club, the club drops to the floor. Quickly he says, "That must be a bad club too . . . give me another substitute." He begins to juggle the three balls. "Ladies and gentlemen, you are now witnessing the famous three-club juggle."

"For my grand finale I will do a trick for you known as multijuggling. All kidding aside folks, this is a very difficult trick which has taken me several years to perfect. I will attempt to juggle for you seven, yes, I said seven, different objects at one time. Many jugglers can juggle three or even four objects at one time, but seven is very hard. Only a few jugglers have ever accomplished it."

He steps over to his prop bag and one by one takes the objects out. "The objects I will juggle include—a football, a club, a cowboy hat, a baloney sandwich, a . . . ??? Wait . . . a baloney sandwich! . . . Forget the sandwich; that's part of my lunch. Now as I was saying a box of cereal, a He-Man masters of the universe toy, a scarf, and a shoe."

"In order to perform this trick I must have your help. I will need absolute silence so that I may have full concentration. So be quiet, please." The juggler acts as if concentrating hard to psyche himself up. He wiggles his fingers rapidly to limber them up. The objects are picked up. "Ready? Here goes." All of the objects are thrown high up above his head. Frantically he tries to catch the first couple of objects as they come down. As the rest descends he screams and ducks, letting all of them land on the floor. He looks up and says in bewilderment, "Why, that's the first time I've dropped those in months," Out of the side of his mouth me adds "That's the first time I've tried that in months.

"Let me attempt it again for you."

Ding, ding. A bell goes off, assistant points to the watch on her arm. "Oh! I see that I'm out of time. Thank you for being a good audience—bye."

HUIDIOT

Props: Trunk or suitcase with the name "Huidiot the Magician" written in big letters across the front, top hat, stuffed rabbit, three trick magic wands, boxing glove, four multiplying sponge balls with two shells.

This is a juggling-magic routine which could be an entire act in itself. The magic wands are the gag type that can go limp. The multiplying balls are the standard sponge ball type sold at magic shops. Inserting a steel ball bearing in each will give them added weight making them easier to juggle. The shells should fit snugly so that they don't come off when thrown into the air. Before going on stage the juggler hides the four balls and the two shells in his pockets.

An MC is required to set the stage for this routine. The act appears to be delayed because the juggler is late. The routine begins as the MC attempts to stall for time.

"Ladies and gentlemen, I'm sorry to announce that our next act has been delayed, so in the meantime, we will—

"Stop, hold it, I'm here, " the juggler yells as he runs up to the stage, obviously out of breath. "Puff, puff, sorry I'm late; I had another show across town and it ran a little late."

"Well, thank goodness you're here now," says the MC. "Let me introduce you. Ladies and gentlemen, I am pleased to introduce to you the great, the one and only, world famous . . . ah . . . ah, what's your name?" MC looks at the trunk the juggler carried up with him and searches for a name on it.

"My name is Dr. Dropo—juggler extraordinaire."

MC, reading the name on the trunk, pronounces it slowly, "Hu-idiot the magician."

"I'm not a magician," the juggler says. "I'm a juggler."

"But your trunk says Huidiot the magician,"

"It does not." The juggler says with a frown. "And stop calling me an idiot. I am a juggler."

"Then why does it say Huidiot the magician?"

Juggler gets mad. "Listen, I'm not a magician and if you call me an idiot one more time, I'll do some magic . . . I'll make your nose swell up like a balloon." Juggler raises his fist.

"No, you don't understand," the MC replies. "If you don't want to be called a magician, Huidiot, why do you have it written on your trunk?"

Juggler puts the trunk down and begins dancing around like a professional boxer. "That does it! I'm going to sock you one good."

"Wait!" MC quickly says. "Look for yourself."

Juggler bends over and reads the words on the trunk. "Oh no, this isn't my trunk. Mine says Dr. Dropo the juggler. This guy was a magician performing at the place I just came from. I must have been in such a hurry that I grabbed his trunk by mistake." Juggler looks apologetic now.

MC frowns. "You IDIOT! Now what are you going to do? I think you ought to keep that trunk; the name is fitting."

"Well . . . ah . . . I know. I can't take it back to the magician right now, I have a show to give. I know, I'll just use the props in this trunk and juggle them."

MC responds. "Well, OK, do what you can."

The juggler opens up the trunk and looks at the contents. "Humm. " Sticking his hand in, he shuffles through the magic equipment. "Let's see, there must be something in here I can juggle." Spotting a top hat he pulls it out. "Hey, look at this, I used to have one of these." Picking it up he holds it over his head and looks inside, as he does a rabbit (stuffed, of course) drops out, smacking him in the nose. "Hey, what was that? Oh . . . it's a rabbit." He tosses the rabbit back into the trunk.

"OK, now watch this." He grabs the rim of the hat between his teeth.

23

He pauses for a few seconds, looking at the audience. Without the use of his hands he flips the hat up and onto his head.

At this point the juggler can perform several hat manipulations. For example, bending his head forward and down towards his right arm, the hat may roll off. It rolls down his arm, end over end into his right hand. The hat is then rotated between the fingers to give a spinning appearance. It is then pushed up into the air with the middle finger and given a spin. The hat spins on the finger much like a basketball would. The juggler then tosses the hat up into the air and catches it in his left hand.

The hat is now sent end over end up the raised left arm, landing back on top of juggler's head. Immediately he tilts his head to the right, transferring the hat to his right arm where it rolls down to his hand. From here it continues off his hand and onto his extended foot. He now kicks the hat up over his head were it lands in place.

Everything is working smoothly. He has just demonstrated some unusual manipulation skills and the audience does not know what to expect next.

The hat is taken off, spun between the fingers, and placed back into the trunk. "Well that was easy enough. What else does he have in here?"

The juggler pulls out three magic wands, "Hey, look here. I can juggle these magic wands." He shows that they are solid by tapping them on the trunk. "I can do a lot of juggling tricks with these."

Just as he attempts to toss one, it goes limp like a noodle. "Hey, what happened?" He tries to straighten it out, but it remains limp. In frustration he starts banging it on the trunk. "Come on now straighten up!" Still it's limp, so he tosses it back into the trunk. "Oh, I'll just juggle these two." As he is about to toss the second wand up into the air it goes limp too. In his other hand the third one drops over like the others. He looks at them with a frown. "Aw, forget it." The wands are thrown back into the trunk.

He looks in the trunk again. "Say, what's this?" He pulls out a boxing glove. "What's a boxing glove doing in here? Is it supposed to be a magic boxing glove or something? What on earth would a

24

magic boxing glove do?"

As he holds it up to the side of his head it whacks him one, WHACK!
"Hey?" WHACK-WHACK. "Hey, cut it out." WHACK-WHACK-
WHACK. "Stop it, stop it!" He grabs the glove with both hands
and wrestles with it. It hits him again—WHACK. He punches it
back—PUNCH. WHACK-PUNCH, WHACK-PUNCH, WHACK-
PUNCH, PUNCH-PUNCH-PUNCH, WHACK-WHACK-WHACK.

Finally he punches and ducks, in retaliation the glove swings and flies
past him onto the floor. Quickly the juggler stamps on it, jumping
up and down. He then stands back to observe its reaction. It just
lies there. He creeps up to it and gives it a timid nudge with his
foot. Nothing happens. He kicks it again. It does not respond.
Deciding that it's dead he reaches down and picks it up. As he stands
up—WHACK, it hits him, then grabs the juggler's throat and begins
choking him.

The juggler grabs the glove and they begin to wrestle. The gloved
is pulled off, but as if a spring were attached to it, the glove flings
back quickly to his face. This is done quickly several times in
succession.

With great effort he pulls the glove away and throws it into the trunk
and slams the lid shut. He stands there with his hands on top of
the trunk for a few seconds to catch his breath. Slowly he opens
the trunk and peaks in. Nothing happens.

He looks around for something else to juggle. "There has got to be
something in here I can juggle. Say, here we go . . . a ball (a
magician's multiplying sponge ball). I wonder if there are any more
in here?" He rummages around for one in the trunk without success.
He takes the ball, which also holds a shell, and looks at the audience.
"I wish I had found another one of these balls and then I could show
you some real fancy juggling."

As he speaks he shows the audience that his hands are empty and
that he holds only a single ball. Suddenly the single ball appears
as two. The juggler looks surprised. "Oh look here, I can do some
juggling. Watch as I juggle, how effortlessly these balls fly through
the air."

25

Juggler clamps them together and throws the ball up in the air. He looks surprised. "Hey, where did the other ball go?" He examines both hands and lets the audience see that now there is only one ball. He continues to look for the second ball. "It's got to be around here somewhere." He pats his shirt pocket then pulls out what appears to be the missing ball. "Here it is. How did it get there? Well, anyway watch this."

Now he shows the audience three balls (two balls and one shell). "Wait a minute. Where did this one come from . . . doesn't matter, it's better this way anyhow. Three ball juggling is more impressive. Now you'll really see some fancy juggling. Watch these three ball—" One ball has now disappeared.

"Hey! Where did the third ball go?" He checks his pockets. "Here it is." The juggler pulls out a third ball. He now has three balls and one shell. The shell is clamped on to one of the balls. The audience sees only three balls.

"Here I go—three ball juggling." The juggler now juggles and does a few different juggling tricks. The final trick: he alternately sticks a ball in his mouth as he juggles. While he's doing this, he pretends to have swallowed one. He swallows, moves his head from side to side and taps his chest lightly. As he does that his face looks sick. He talks with a rasping voice. "I . . . I think I swallowed it."

He holds up the two balls concealing the third. "I will just juggle two balls—" He looks at his hand and there are four balls (three balls and one shell). He does a double take. "Huh? Four balls, how did that happen? Oh well . . . ah, I will juggle four balls then. This is very difficult, much more so then juggling three. The ability to juggle four balls separates the common juggler from the true professional. Hold onto your seats for this—"

He looks at his hand and finds only three balls. The shell is clamped onto one of the three balls. "What, only three again? Now that I built you up for my four ball juggling demonstration, I'm missing one. Let's see, where would it have gone?"

He checks his pockets and as he does, he secretly palms one ball and one shell and pulls them out of his pocket. "Not there—CHOKE!"

He makes a funny face, stretches his neck around and grabs his mouth with the hand holding the palmed ball and shell. Opening his mouth it appears as if he expels the palmed ball out of it. He shows a surprised look on his face, looks at the ball and then at the audience, back at the ball and again at the audience and shrugs his shoulders. "Well I've got my fourth ball back now, so I will continue."

His face suddenly looks sick again. His tongue pushes against his cheek to make it appear as if he has something in his mouth. Grabbing his mouth he pulls out what appears to be a fifth ball but is actually the palmed shell. This is done with a lot of facial expression. The four balls and shell are put into one hand and shown to the audience. The second shell is palmed in the other hand.

Again the juggler's face looks sick. He grabs his mouth, pushes his cheeks out with his tongue and pulls out the shell making it look like an ordinary ball. The four balls and two shells are then arranged between his fingers to show the audience six balls.

Suddenly his face looks sick again. He hits his chest as if he has heartburn, "This is getting ridiculous." His tongue pushes against his cheek. He reaches up to pull what everyone thinks will be another ball, but he just sticks out his tongue. Grabbing the tongue he gives it a pull. "Ouch! Oh . . . it's just my tongue Well I've got six balls here so I will attempt to juggle all six. This is a feat [feet] rarely seen because I usually keep my shoes on. ' The juggler waits for audience to catch on to joke.

Before tossing the balls, the two shells are clamped onto two of the balls so that there are only four balls in the juggler's hand. The juggler throws the balls in the air and juggles the four balls. Although he is only juggling four balls it is hard for the audience to determine how many he is actually using. If juggled for only a short time, the audience will believe he actually did juggle six balls.

The juggler stops, separates the shells, and again shows the audience six balls. He signals for an applause then opens the case to deposit the balls. As he does, the boxing glove jumps out and grabs him. He fights with the glove and tosses it back inside the case, slamming the lid shut.

MONSTER BALLS

Props: Three balls all of the same color, such as red. One green clay ball of the same size. One green beach ball. One medical type bag, lipstick tube, one bottle of 7-UP, trick drinking glass (optional), x-ray machine (box with lights), tape recording of mechanical noise which will be the sound caused by the x-ray machine.

For this routine two performers are needed. One will play the juggler and the other will play the doctor. The routine is best described in dialog form. The "J" stands for juggler and "D" for doctor (Dr. Dropo).

The routine starts off with the juggler coming into the doctor's office. With him are his two juggling balls and the green clay ball, which is sick.

J: Doctor, I've brought my juggling balls into you for a check-up. I think one of them is sick.
D: Why do you think it is sick?
J: Well up until a day or two ago this ball (hold up green ball) used to be the same color as these others. (Show two other red balls.)
D: Oh I don't think that's anything to worry about.
J: But there's more doctor . . . watch. (He starts to juggle the balls. The green ball goes in different patterns from that of the other two. Some of the juggling patterns might be *columns, over the top*, and *under the arm*.) Wait that's not all, look at this. (Bounce the first two balls on the floor, *floor bounce*, then throw the green ball down. Being made of clay it will hit and remain on the floor.) See Doc, it's just not the same as it used to be.
D: Yes, I see what you mean. Well I suggest you take this ball to the doctor and have it examined.
J: Why, that's a good idea, thank you, see you later Doc. Hey . . . wait a minute, that's the reason why I'm here to see you.
D: Well you made a wise decision young man because I, Dr. Dropo.am one of the best musicians in this city.
J: Musician? I thought musicians were people who played musical instruments.
D: Oh, did I say musician? I must have meant magician. I am one of the best magicians in this city.
J: Magician? Isn't a magician a person who does magic, you know like making things disappear?

28

D: Yeah, I guess you're right; I wish I could disappear right now.

J: Isn't the word you're looking for, physician?

D: Physician? . . . What's that?

J: A physician is a doctor, so you should have said you are one of the best physicians in this entire city.

D: Well that's what I've been trying to tell you boy, I'm famous for my medical skills. Now let me have a look at that ball. (Doctor takes the sick ball into his hand.) Open you mouth and say "ahh."

J: Ahh.

D: No, not you, the ball.

J: Oh, sorry.

D: Well, I think the problem is that he needs to go on a diet. How much does he eat each day?

J: Why nothing . . . I don't feed him. He doesn't eat anything. How can he be overweight?

D: Hmm . . . that's a good point. Maybe he's not getting enough to eat, try feeding him more.

J: What do you suggest I feed him, doctor?

D: Well, let's see, hmm . . . If I were a little rubber ball what would I like to eat? . . . Try pickles and peanut butter sandwiches; that's my favorite.

J: But Doc, I don't think balls are supposed to eat anything, they don't even have mouths.

D: Yes, I guess you're right. Well . . . bring him over here and let me run some more tests on him. (Picks up a hammer and proceeds to hit the ball.)

J: Doctor! What are you doing?

D: Oh, I'm just testing his reflexes. I think I will need some x-rays. I'll just put him into the x-ray machine and turn the power on high.

J: Doc, why are you turning the power up so high? It's only a little ball; won't it get an overdose of radiation?

D: Nah, I turn it up high for all my patients. Now stand back while I turn this thing on. (Turns x-ray machine on; lights flashing and noise indicate the machine is working.) OK, now let me take the little feller out of there. OH NO! We used too much radiation . . . look what it did to your ball. (Pull out beach ball.)

J: AAH! My ball what's happened to it?

D: We've given it too much radiation in the x-ray machine. It's grown to an abnormally large size and it's still growing! . . . It will soon be as large as the Astrodome. I can see it all now, new movies from Japan titled "Attack of the Giant Juggling Ball" or "Monster

Juggling Ball Versus Godzilla."

J: Can't you do something, Doc? Don't you have an antidote or something?

D: I don't know, let me look in my medical bag . . . ah, yes, here try this.

J: What is it?

D: I don't know, it just says Passion Pink.

J: Wait, what does it say on the other side?

D: Lipstick by Avon . . . oh, I think we better try something else.

J: Yes I think so.

D: Here try this.

J: What is it?

D: It's a bottle of 7-UP.

J: SEVEN-UP! Why are you giving him that?

D: I don't know, but it helps my stomach feel better when it's upset and I bet your juggling ball's stomach is really upset by now. (Give the ball a drink. Trick glass works good here. Use the type that looks full and appears to empty as it is titled.) There now, let's set him down for awhile to rest. (Put ball out of site next to the third red Ball.)

J: I sure hope this works.

D: Let's take a look and see how he's doing.

J: (Reaches in and picks up a red juggling ball.) It worked! He's back to his normal size again. Doc you're a genius. (Juggler starts juggling and performs several tricks without any problem.) You did it, Doc, he's all well again. (Walks off stage juggling. Doc just stands there scratching his head in surprise.)

THEY CALL ME STUBBY

Props: Three juggling knives.

"I just happen to have some knives (pronounced ka-nives) that's right ka-nives. You see, I can't say knives so I have to say ka-nives."

"I need a volunteer, how about you . . . come up here please." Spectator comes up on the stage. Juggler asks his new helper a few questions such as: "What's your name? How old are you? Do you have any brothers or sisters? What grade are you in? Have you ever helped a juggler before? Do you know how to juggle. Are you married?

What do you do for a living?"

"Do you know why I asked you to come up here?"

"No."

"I asked you to come up here so that I could teach you to juggle. Would you like that?"

"Yes."

"Good. We'll start by juggling these knives. Have you ever juggled knives before?"

"No."

"Me either, that's why I'm having YOU do it . . . OK, Tom (or what ever the helper's name is) I have two questions for you before we start. First (pointing to knife) what's this?"

"A knife."

"Right, and what's this?" Juggler points to his thumb and wiggles it.

"Your thumb."

"Right again, my thumb. Please don't forget the difference because knives are sharp! To show you and the audience how sharp they arc, look what this knife does to this carrot." The carrot is hit against the blade of the knife slicing it up. This will work no matter now dull the knife is.

"Now I'm going to teach you to juggle knives so that when you get home you can show the kids on your block how well you can juggle or how stubby your fingers are—whichever comes first. To juggle a knife all you need to do is just toss it in the air like this see . . . Oooh!" Juggler catches bladed part of knife and makes painful face.

"I want you to watch me closely so that you will be able to repeat what I do. I'm now going to juggle three knives. As I do so I will throw one of them high up into the air and when it comes down I will catch it with my teeth." He turns to Tom. "Watch very closely because I'm going to have you do it next."

"These knives are very sharp and you must be very accurate or bloodshed will result." Juggler begins to juggle the knives. One is tossed high up in the air. He looks up at it, steps forward, and opens his mouth as if to let it drop in. He continues to step forward and the knife drops behind him. "You know the last time I did this trick a lady in the front row fainted."

He picks up the knife and juggles all three again. He tosses one high up in the air. Opening his mouth he leans forward under the falling knife. As it comes down he pulls his head back to let the knife drop to the floor. "I used to have a friend who did this trick. Funny, he only did it once . . . rest his soul."

Once again he begins to juggle the knives. He fakes like he tosses one of the knives up and just places the knife in his mouth. "Ta-da . . . did you see it? Would you like to see it again?"

"Yes," they say.

"A good magician shows his audience his tricks only once . . . But I'm a lousy magician so I'll show you again." He juggles the knives, throws one up, bends to catch it with his teeth. As he does, the knife misses his mouth and he pretends to have been stabbed in the chest. "Oooh!" He staggers around. "Is there a doctor in the house?" He stands up pulls the knife out. "Just kidding."

HAIRY HARRY

Props: Mouse hand puppet, carrying case for puppet, three juggling balls, three foam rubber hammers.

This is an excellent routine for kids. The juggler uses a hand puppet and a ventriloquist-type dialog. The "H" stands for Harry and "J" for juggler.

J: I would like to introduce to you a friend of mine. He is actually more of a pet then a friend. His name is Harry and he's my pet mouse. This isn't any ordinary mouse, mind you, this mouse can juggle. Yes, that's right, he is a juggling mouse. Let me have him come out so you can meet him. (Open the carrying case.) Harry . . . it's time to come out now.

H: Oh good, it was getting stuffy in there . . . oh, look at all the kids. Hi, kids!

J: Harry, I told the kids you would do some juggling for them.

H: I can't do that!

J: Why not?

H: I don't know how to juggle.

J: Oh you do so. You're a very good juggler. You can juggle balls, clubs, apples and all sorts of things. You're an expert juggler, almost as good as I am.

H: Gosh, Dr. Dropo, you really think so.

J: Sure. Here show the kids what you can do . . . juggle these two balls. (Dropo gives Harry two juggling balls.)

H: OK. (Harry juggles both balls catching them in his mouth which is actually the juggler's hand.)

J: Good Harry, now let's juggle as a team. I'll get another ball, and we will juggle all three. Ya ready?

H: Ready.

J: Let's go. (Harry and Dropo do three ball cascade and a few simple tricks such as *columns*, *over the top*, etc.) All right, let's do some bouncing tricks.

H: How about the elbow bounce where we bounce the ball off your elbow.

J: OK. I'll do it first. (Dropo does an *elbow bounce*.) Now it's your turn, you try it Harry.

H: OK, here goes. (Harry tosses a ball up and it comes down on Dropo's head.)

J: Ouch! . . . Hey what's the big idea?

H: It slipped.

J: Oh all right, let's try it again, the *elbow bounce* . . . (Ball hits Dropo on the head again.) OUCH! You knucklehead. Why did you do that?

H: I thought it was funny so I did it again. Didn't you think it was funny, kids?

J: Well, I didn't. So don't do it again. Let's try another trick.

H: How about the knee bounce?

J: Yeah, that's a good trick—here let me do it first—

H: How come you always get to go first?

J: Because I'm the star of the show and you're just my dumb assistant.

H: Well, I want to go first this time, you always get to. (Next seven lines are said in quick succession.)

J: No!

H: Please.

J: No!

H: Please.

J: No!

H: please.

J: NOOOOOO! . . . Now let's go. This, kids, is the *knee bounce*. (Dropo does *knee bounce* a couple of times on his left knee.) OK, Harry, now you try it. Toss the ball up and be sure you hit right on top of my knee so it will bounce back up properly. (Dropo says this while pointing to his left knee.)

H: Toss it right on top of your knee you say?

J: That's right.

H: OK, here goes. (Harry slams a ball into Dropo's knee.)

J: Ouch! . . . I don't mean now, wait until I'm ready. (Dropo picks up the ball and starts to juggle.) Now, Harry, toss it. (Dropo lifts his left knee but Harry throws the ball on top of Dropo's right foot.) OW! . . . Harry, what's the big idea?

H: I thought you were going to lift the other knee up.

J: (Dropo shakes his head.) All right let's try it again. (They juggle again, but this time Dropo lifts his right leg and Harry drops the ball on to Dropo's left foot.) OW! . . . What did you do that for!

H: I thought you wanted me to toss it to your other leg.

J: Forget this trick, let's do another one. Let's do the one where we toss all three balls one at a time behind my back and up over my shoulder (*behind the back toss*) where we will grab them and continue juggling.

H: All right.

J: Let me go first—

H: Wait a minute, you went first the last couple of times; it's my turn to go first.

J: You can't go first Harry you might ah . . . mess up or something. (Harry and Dropo say the following six lines in quick succession.)

H: Please.

J: No!

H: Please.

J: No!

H: please.

J: NOOOO!

H: (Harry, angry now, purposely drops all the balls on the floor.)

J: Harry, What did you do that for?

H: If you won't let me go first, I'm not going to juggle with you.

J: But every time I let you go first, you always mess up.

H: I won't this time, I've been practicing.

J: Oh, all right, you go first. Remember we're tossing all three balls back behind my back and over my shoulder. Let me see you do a practice toss first.

H: OK. (Harry tosses one ball behind Dropo and up over his shoulder performing the *behind the back toss*.)

J: All right, that was good, let's go (Dropo and Harry start to juggle.) OK, Harry do it. (Harry throws the balls up and hits Dropo in the head with each of them.) Ouch—ouch—ouch! . . . Harry, you numbskull, what do you think you're doing hitting me in the head and dropping all the balls?

H: Well, if your head wasn't in the way I could have done the trick and you wouldn't have dropped the balls.

J: If *my* head wasn't in the way, I wouldn't have dropped the balls!

H: That's right, that's just what I said too.

J: (Dropo is mad now.) I didn't drop those balls, you clumsy oaf, you did. What did you expect me to do, catch those balls with my teeth?

H: Why not, I do. In fact, that takes more skill than catching them with your hands like you do. Ya know, my mother told me not to take you on as my partner because you were too clumsy.

J: Me, clumsy?

H: Yes, I agree. You big over-grown turnip. Why, if you could ever—

J: (At this point Dropo crams a ball into Harry's mouth.)

H: Gag . . . why . . . mumble mumble . . . you—

J: (Dropo sticks the other two balls into his mouth.)

H: Mumble, mumble.

J: There that ought to shut you up, ha ha.

H: Mumble, mumble.

J: What was that, Harry?

H: Mumble, mumble, garble.

J: I can't understand you, speak up.

H: (Harry screams as loud as he can with his mouth stuffed up.) Mumble, garble, gook!

J: I can't understand a word you're saying. (Dropo takes the balls out of Harry's mouth.) What did you say?

H: (Harry looks at him with a frown and growls.) Grrr. You know Dropo, there is one thing I think would be awful funny to juggle.

J: What's that Harry?

H: Your nose. (Harry grabs Dropo's nose in his mouth and shakes it.)

J: Hey, what's the—(This is said with a nasal voice.)

H: (Harry releases Dropo's nose, makes a sour face, and spits as if he just tasted something bad.) Pewhy, pewhy, yuck.

J: Hey, what's the big idea, you rat.

H: Now don't bring my family into this.

J: OK, OK. We're running out of time, and we've got one last trick to show the kids.

H: You mean the hammers?

J: Yes, the hammers. (Dropo faces audience.) Harry and I will now juggle three large hammers.

H: Are those hammers for real?

J: Why sure they are, look. (Dropo hits Harry over the head with one.)

H: Ouch! . . . That wasn't funny.

J: Well, the kids thought so.

H: Hmm . . . so they did, that gives me an idea.

J: What's that?

H: Oh, nothing. I was just talking to myself.

J: All right let's go. (As they begin to juggle Harry hits Dropo in the stomach with one of the hammers. Dropo makes a funny face. Harry hits him again on top of his head.) Ooo . . . ouch . . . hey, that wasn't funny.

H: Well, the kids thought so.

LIVER JUICE AND OTHER DELIGHTS

Props: Three balls, two of one color one of another. Large medicine bottle, box to rest ball in, tape recording of loud munching sound, one juggling club.

The theme to this routine is similar to Monster Balls described earlier. A juggler is bringing his sick juggling ball in for the doctor to examine. The "D" is for doctor and the "J" for juggler.

J: Doctor, I'm here to see you because I have a ball that is sick.

D: You what?

J: I am a juggler by profession and one of my juggling balls is acting up, I think it's sick.

D: What seems to be the trouble with it?

J: Well . . . here, you try it and see what happens.

D: OK, (Doctor does a few tricks in which the sick ball goes in different patterns than the others, such as in *columns, over the top*, etc. This is followed by bouncing the sick ball of his head.) Ouch! (Finally doctor's head is moved out of the way, letting the odd ball drop inside of his open shirt or coat. Doctor gives a surprised look on his face.) Hey, what are you doing in there? (He opens up his shirt collar to look in.) Stop hiding and come on out. (He reaches in to grab it.) Oh, don't you run away from me; come here. (Doctor bends over, reaches deep into his shirt and starts to spin in a circle as if chasing the ball.) Come here, you!

J: Here, let me help you. (The juggler reaches into the doctor's shirt, looking for the ball.)

D: Ho ho hee ha ha, cut that out; I'm ticklish.

J: There, I got it. Well what do you think, Doc, is he sick?

D: Yes, I think you're right; it doesn't act normally. I have something which will make it better in no time. (Doctor pulls out a bottle of medicine.) Here give him some of this.

J: What is it?

D: It's a medicine I invented to cure all sorts of ailments. It will cure measles, scurvy, chicken pox, restore hair, remove warts, straighten crooked teeth, and relieve gas. Most any type of problem you have, it will cure.

J: Yeah, but can it cure my juggling ball?

D: We can give it a try and see. (Starts to give the ball a drink.)

J: What's in this medicine that makes it so powerful.

D: Oh, many things. It's got prune juice, caster oil, peanut butter, raw eggs, polyunsaturated pig fat, sesame seed pulp, liver extract, avocados, and a pinch of lemon juice. A combination of many healthy foods.

J: Yuck! That sounds terrible, how do you get anyone to drink that mess?

D: I don't know—no one has ever tried it before.

J: But you just said it cured all ills.

D: It does, anybody who has come to me complaining of a sickness is miraculously healed when I bring it out and try to give it to them. Why just the other day a man who had been crippled from birth leaped up and ran out of my office when I tried to give him a drink.

J: But, Doctor—

D: Don't worry, your juggling ball can't run away, so we will give it a snort. (Doctor tries to give the ball a drink, but it refuses and puts up a fight. The ball and the doctor wrestle around the room, on the table, then the floor. Finally the ball swallows the medicine. There it's done; let me put it over here (inside a box) to rest while the medicine takes effect.

J: I hope this works Doc. He's been terrible to live with these last few days.

D: Let's take a look and see how our patient is doing. (Doctor looks into the box where the ball is resting.) OH NO! . . . I was afraid something like this would happen. Look what happened to your ball. (Pulls out a juggling club.)

J: Ahh . . . what's happened to it? It's grown out of proportion. How can I ever juggle a thing like this? Is there anything you can do to change it back?

D: I don't think so. Why don't you just try juggling it; maybe it won't be as bad as you think.

J: OK. (Juggler juggles two balls and the club.) Maybe this won't be too bad. It doesn't bounce very well though. (Throws the club on floor.)

D: Here let me try it. (Doctor starts to juggle them but club keeps hitting him on the head.) Ouch ouch ouch!

J: It's still not cured, Doc, what can you do?

D: Let me think . . . I've got it. Since my medicine was made of a bunch of healthy foods maybe if we give it a bunch of junk food it will offset the healthy food. (Puts club back into box.) Here let's try this and this and some of this. (Put candy bars, soda, chips, ice cream, etc. into box and play recording of loud munching sound. When the noise stops, the Doctor pulls out the original ball, all cured.) Here you are, try this.

J: (The juggler then juggles and performs several tricks without problems.) Thanks, Doctor, you're a genius.

LOVE AND MARRIAGE

Props: Three juggling rings, tape recording of fog horn or some similar sound, three juggling balls, two juggling clubs, one fake bowling ball.

"Ya know, love is a funny thing. It makes people do the strangest

38

things . . . like getting married. I just got married a few weeks ago. A person has to make a lot of changes in his life when he gets married. Before I got married, I used to go bowling four times a week, but not any more. My wife won't let me. Reminds me of an old saying." Performer picks up bowling ball and two juggling clubs and juggles them. To most people juggling clubs look like bowling pins. "Balls and pins, balls and pins, when a man marries, his trouble begins . . . Isn't that the truth.

"Before we were married she told me she wouldn't marry me when I was drunk, but I told her I wouldn't marry her when I was sober.

"She's quite an emotional woman. She says every time she thinks about our wedding, she cries. Every time I think about our wedding, I cry.

"We went to a real pretty church for our wedding. The windows were stained glass, but they washed them for the wedding.

"I think I must have been sober when I got married. My bride walked down the aisle and her father and three brothers helped me down the aisle.

"The minister said the words, 'Forgive them for they know not what they do' . . . or whatever they say at weddings.

"I had gone out and purchased a ring for her that morning and I pulled it out." Juggler pulls out one of the large juggling rings. "And said I wasn't sure of your size, I hope it fits . . . it did.

"You know marriage is a three ring circus." Juggler picks up all three rings, one at a time, and juggles them. "First you have the engagement ring. Then comes the wedding ring, and then finally the suffering." Juggler puts rings down.

"The ring I bought fit just right. Really my wife is a dainty little thing . . . compared to Moby Dick.

"She's also a very talented woman. You may have seen her on TV; she played the part of Godzilla in those monster movies. Her director said she had a great future in motion pictures because she didn't have to waste time putting on makeup. Isn't it amazing how long it takes a woman to put on her makeup? Whenever we go out to the movies, we try to hit the double feature because by the time she gets her makeup on, we're late and we've missed the first show. I guess it's worth it, though. She says she puts on makeup to make her look decent, and let me tell you, without the makeup, she really looks indecent.

"You guys who are married, have you ever noticed how your money has dwindled since you got married? I think when women get married they feel it's an obligation to get rid of our hard earned money as fast as we make it. On pay days when I come home, my wife always greets me at the door with these friendly words," Juggler picks up three balls and does three ball *claws*. "'Give me, give me, give me.'

"Semi . . . that's my wife's name. I think they named her after a truck. Semi, she's really a nice woman. She says she wants to name our first child after me—Jerky.

"My wife tells me I'm lazy. I'm not really, it just looks that way because I sit around a lot . . . well, I have to. To conserve energy for my bowling.

"She says to me, 'Worm', (that's what my wife calls me) 'Worm' (juggler speaks in a high pitched voice) 'all you ever do is sit around, why don't you do anything? When we got married and I said, 'I do', I didn't know it meant I do the cooking, I do the cleaning, I do the laundry, I do the yard work, I do this, I do that, I do everything.' We're really happily married; at least that's what she tells me to say."

Recording of fog horn is played. "Oh, I have to go now, that's my wife calling me." Performer yells to wife, "Yes, dear, I'm coming."

WUN DARN LI

Props: Three juggling clubs, trunk or suitcase, recording of mysterious or magic type music, loose pants with hidden pocket, two small rubber balls and one matching non-bouncing ball, a set of large magic linking rings, two red juggling scarves, one blue juggling scarf, one yellow juggling scarf, thumb tip.

For this juggling-magic routine, some magic props are needed, like

40

the thumb tip and linking rings. Details on how to work these are supplied by the manufacturer and will not be discussed here. The pants need to be slightly baggy, like a warm up suit. A pocket just large enough to hold one of the juggling balls (the smaller the balls the better) is sewn inside behind where a belt buckle would be located. A belt should not be used but the pants should have an elastic band, like sweat pants.

Before coming out on stage, the juggler has placed two balls under the elastic band of his pants behind his back. These are concealed from the audience. The juggler comes on stage carrying a trunk or suitcase and three juggling clubs or rings.

The routine starts with the juggler performing some club or ring juggling. After doing a few tricks he puts the props away.

"I would like to show you some magic now. The reason for the magic, is that people like to see it, and when I perform they often ask if I can do any magic. Up till now, I would tell them no. But I met a fine old Chinese gentleman at one of the shows I was at recently. He was a retired magician. Grew up doing Vaudeville magic shows and was quite popular.

"He offered to sell me all of his old magic supplies since he didn't need them any more. He said all his magic supplies were in excellent condition and would make me a good deal, told me his name was Wun Darn Li. He offered them to me for only a fraction of their cost. I couldn't resist and bought his whole trunk full of magic props.

"Since I just bought this trunk yesterday, I don't even know what all is in here. I haven't had much time to practice the magic, so I will do some magic juggling for you. Looking through the trunk I did find this ball, which will fit right in to my juggling act."

Mysterious sounding music is played now to set the atmosphere. Juggler tosses the single ball up and down. It is bounced off his elbow, leg, foot, and arm.

He now juggles the ball with one hand, alternately tossing and catching it with the back of his hand, then the palm. As he does this, his left hand rests on his hip and secretly pulls out a ball which was hidden behind his back. With his hand behind his back, he flicks the ball

41

up over his shoulder so that it appears to the audience as if it came from nowhere. He grabs it and begins juggling both balls in his left hand. His right hand now rests on his right hip. Secretly he removes the other ball hidden behind his back. It is tossed up like the other one was. The ball goes up over his shoulder and he juggles all three balls.

The juggler performs various three ball juggling moves. The music, which is still playing, adds enchantment and mystery.

One ball is held in the left hand and two are juggled in the right. These balls are thrown high into the air. The third ball, which is held casually near the navel, is secretly slipped into the hidden pocket. The small size of the ball and the looseness of the pants conceal the ball.

After hiding the ball, the juggler catches one of the other two balls with the left hand and begins juggling the two balls in his left hand. He opens his right hand to show the audience that he only has two balls now and signals by holding up two fingers. The balls are shifted to his right hand and juggled. The left hand is opened and shown to contain no hidden ball. He then begins to juggle the two balls between both hands. As he does, he slowly pivots. As his back faces the audience he secretly removes the hidden ball and tosses it up with the other two so that when the turn is completed he is juggling three balls. To show the audience that he clearly has three balls he does *column* juggling.

The juggler bounces the two rubber balls on the floor as he juggles. Several other bouncing type tricks are done such as the *knee bounce* and the *arm bounce*. This shows that all the balls are normal bouncing type balls.

Taking the non-bouncing ball he does a knee bounce, hitting it hard so that it rebounds high up into the air. As it is flung into the air, the juggler takes his free hand and zaps the ball with his fingers. An unseen force has been sent from his fingers into the ball. What he did was to put a magic spell on the ball so that it loses all of its bounce. When the ball hits the ground it will stay put. The audience just saw the juggler bounce that very same ball off his knee so they know that it was bounceable. How it lost its bounce is a mystery to them. He picks up the ball but drops it on the floor to show that it is dead. He now drops it on this knee but refrains from hitting it with much force so that the ball hits and rolls off onto the floor. The audience is convinced the ball has lost its bounce.

The juggler tosses the ball high up into the air. Again he raises his hand and zaps it with an unseen force. The ball's bounce has now been restored. As the ball comes down, it is bounced off his knee and juggling is resumed. All three balls are bounced off various parts of the body. Floor bounces are also performed to show the audience that all the balls can now bounce.

The music is stopped and the juggler begins to talk as he casually juggles. "I used no tricks or gimmicks to perform this exquisite display of magic juggling. Just superior skill, coordination, and my natural magical forces. Yes, that's right, I kid you not. May my right arm become paralyzed if I'm not telling the truth." His right arm immediately stiffens up and sticks out toward the audience. "AHHHHH!" Two balls are continuously bounced from the extended arm to his left hand. The third ball is held in the right hand. He shakes his arm and it loosens up again.

"Let me try something else." He goes into the trunk. "Hey, look what I found." He pulls out two large magic linking rings. "I've seen magicians use these, haven't you? They make these rings pass through each other and link up." As he says this, he tries to push the two rings together, but they won't go. He becomes frustrated and hits them against each other.

"Stupid rings . . . don't work, no wonder I got them so cheaply. Hmm . . . even if I can't do any magic with them I can juggle them. You may have seen jugglers juggle rings before. Although these are not juggling type rings, it shouldn't be any different. I'll need another one if I'm going to juggle them."

He looks into the trunk and secretly replaces the two rings he had and pulls out the key ring and three connected rings. "Hey, I found two more! I'll show you some four ring juggling." He holds the key ring in his right hand and the others in his left. They are separated slightly to make them appear unattached. Holding them closely together with both hands he continues. "I will now juggle four rings."

The key ring is linked to the others and all of them are tossed up

43

into the air. He holds onto the key ring but lets the others fly up. He screams, "YEKS! . . . They're all stuck together. They weren't like that before. I can't juggle them like this."

He grabs hold of the rings with both hands and tugs on them. "Come apart, you!" He wrestles around with them trying to separate them. As he fights, they are linked into various configurations which the audience can see. He becomes more and more frustrated.

"Stupid things just won't cooperate." Finally he gives up. "I'm sorry folks I just can't seem to get them separated." As he says that he pulls the key ring free and slightly separates the others to give the appearance that they are now all unattached. "What? They're free . . . OK, now I can juggle them for you." Again he attempts to juggle them by throwing them up into the air. Like before, he has connected the key ring so that they are all attached again. "YEKS! . . . What's this . . . they're stuck together again."

He grabs them and tries to pull them apart. After wrestling around with them for a few seconds he holds them up and shows two rings linked. He pulls on one but it just hits against the side of the other one. Secretly he disconnects the key ring. Holding the free ring close to one of the others, he slides it along as if trying to pull it off just as he tried before. To his utter surprise it slips right off.

"What? How did that happen?" He than pushes the two rings back together, trying to link them, but they won't go. As he fumbles with it, the ring is reattached without his realizing how. He is totally frustrated now.

"I give up folks, these things won't separate." As he says that he pulls the key ring off and separates the other three slightly. "Oh I don't care if they are apart now, I'm putting them back."

He puts them back into the trunk and begins to turn away when a thought crosses his mind. "Say, maybe I was just trying to juggle too many of them. Perhaps I could juggle them if I only use three."

With that he reaches in and pulls out the key ring and two separated rings. "Before I start let me make sure these are all separated." He then holds up each ring one at a time. "OK here we go." The rings remain separated and he is able to juggle with them. He smiles with accomplishment. A trick is done by bouncing a ring off the floor as he juggles. With a little practice you can make the large rings bounce.

He grabs the rings and says, "OK, now that I've got them to juggle, I will do some tricks for you. The first trick I will do will be to take these rings, swing them behind my back, up over my shoulder where I will catch and juggle them."

The key ring is linked to the other two so that as they're swung behind his back, they stick together and appear to smack into the back of the juggler's head. "OUCH! What the . . . ? They're stuck together again . . . that does it, forget this trick." He tosses the rings back into the trunk.

Turning back to the trunk he searches inside and finds a red scarf. As he pulls the scarf out he palms the thumb tip. Three scarves of different colors, which have been tied together, are secretly stuffed up the juggler's sleeve. Pulling the red scarf out, he holds it up to show the audience. He shows both sides. Holding the thumb tip in his left hand he stuffs the scarf into his closed left fist. Miraculously the scarf has now vanished. He opens his hand to show the audience it's empty. The juggler proceeds to look in a couple of pockets as if searching for the scarf. The thumb tip and scarf is deposited in one of these pockets. Looking in his sleeve he notices the tip of a red scarf dangling out slightly. He grabs it an slowly pulls it out. The yellow one is loosely tied to the end of the red, so he keeps pulling till the yellow scarf comes out. The blue scarf is tied to the end of the yellow one and it too is pulled out of the sleeve. The audience is shown three scarves all attached. He unties them.

"I will now do a trick which defies the laws of nature. The magical force within my fingers will zap these scarves and they will become totally weightless and float motionless in mid-air. The old Chinese magician Wun Darn Li told me this trick worked for him every the time."

He takes the three scarves and throws them as high in the air as he can. He points his fingers at one and says, "ZAP!". . . Nothing happens, the scarf just floats down towards the ground. He zaps it again and again, nothing happens. By this time the scarves are drifting toward the floor so he quickly grabs them and throws them back up.

He zaps the first one again, then the second, and then the third. They continue to float down to the floor. He is mad now and zaps one but quickly grabs it and tosses it up in the air again. He zaps another and tosses it into the air again. He zaps the third and throws it back up. The first scarf is getting close to the ground so he quickly grabs it and tosses it up.

He continues to grab and toss the scarves up without regard to any juggling pattern. He runs around, back and forth, all over the stage trying to keep the scarves afloat. Finally, in exhaustion, he slows down and the scarves settle on the floor. He wipes his brow and puffs, out of breath. "That's all, folks"

THE KLUTZY MECHANIC

Props: Three juggling balls, two of one color and one of another. Oil can, large screwdriver, large uninflated balloon the same color as the single ball, one juggling club the same color as the balloon, three juggling rings.

This skit uses two performers. One plays the mechanic, the other a juggler. The basic idea is that the juggler is bringing in his juggling balls for a tune-up. The "J" is for Juggler, "M" is for mechanic.

J: I have been having some trouble with this ball lately. Could you give it a tune-up?

M: What seems to be the problem?

J: Well, here, try it out and see for yourself.
   M: (Mechanic juggles three balls. The odd colored ball does something different from the other two. Tricks may include: *columns*, *over the top*, alternating *under arm*, etc.) It doesn't seem to follow the others very well, does it?

J: That's not all; try bouncing it off your knee.

M: OK. (Mechanic attempts the *knee bounce* and lifts up his knee but the ball drops on his head.) OW!

J: You see, it just won't cooperate. I think something must be wrong with it.
   M: I think I know what's wrong. I think it has a screw loose— let me tighten it . . . there. Now let's see if that helped out. (Mechanic starts to juggle them again but this time the odd ball

continually slaps him in the face.) OUCH . . . OUCH . . . OUCH!

J: It didn't work.

M: Maybe all it needs is some grease. (Mechanic pulls out oil can and oils the ball.) There now, here, try it and see how it works.

J: OK. (Juggler grabs the ball.) YUCK! (Juggler makes ugly face and wipes oil off hand onto his pants. He juggles balls and as he does, the odd one is tossed sideways and hits mechanic in back of his head.)

M: OUCH!

J: No, that didn't do it either.

M: Here give it to me. (Mechanic puts the ball on a table out of sight of audience. He uses a hammer, saw, and wrench as he works on it. Finally he uses a screwdriver. Pretending to twist something he slips nozzle of balloon over end of screwdriver. He now begins to fight with it. Holding down one end of the balloon and lifting up on the nozzle end with the screwdriver, he pulls up, it pulls down. They fight up and down, up and down, up and down. Finally he releases the balloon as he is pulling up and the balloon snaps him in the face.) OOOOUCH! (Picking the balloon up with two fingers he hands it to the juggler.) There, that ought to do it.

J: (Juggler looks with shock.) WHAT! . . . what did you do to my ball? I can't juggle it like this.

M: Why not?

J: Well . . . It's too small and wiggly.

M: Oh, all right, give it here. (Mechanic pulls out some more tools and works on it some more. Tools he uses include: air pump, hedge clippers, and saw.) OK, here . . . try it now. (Mechanic hands juggler a juggling club.)

J: EEK! . . . What have you done to my ball!?

M: Well, you see it's A frame was bent and I had to replace that with a fragma-gagit, but it was too short so I lengthened the wrench-snoggles to fit over the harborator so the baily-ratchet would slide on.

J: (Juggler has puzzled look.) Oh?. . . Yeah, sure, of course.

M: Here, try it.

J: OK. (Juggler now does two balls one club juggling and tricks without problems.) Hey. . . I think you did fix it, it's working just fine now, OUCH . . . OUCH . . . OUCH. (Club hits juggler repeatedly on head as he juggles.) This won't do, I want it to look like a ball, like it did before.

M: Well . . . OK, I'll see what I can do. (Mechanic puts the club on the table and starts to work on it.) Hmm, I'll need to see one of your other balls to make sure I get the correct size.

J: OK, here. (Juggler hands him one of the other balls.)

M: (He works on both balls for a while.) Oh oh.

J: (Juggler looks worried.) What's wrong?

M: (Mechanic is embarrassed.) Oh nothing . . . nothing as all . . . ahh . . . could I see that other ball of yours?

J: Yeah, sure, here.

M: (Mechanic works on all three balls.) Well, this is about as good as I can do for you. (He hands juggler one juggling ring.)

J: What did you do with my ball!? (Juggler grabs ring to examine it.) How am I going to juggle this thing with my other two balls? . . . It won't match.

M: Oh, don't worry, I fixed that, here. (He hands juggler two more rings.) I fixed them to look just like the first.

J: WHAT!!! How am I going to use these?

M: Just try it, you'll like it—I'm sure of it.

J: (Juggler juggles rings.) Say, this isn't too bad . . . I think I do like it. Thanks. (Juggler walks off stage juggling.)

GOOFY MOOFY OR
HOW TO KEEP BALLS OFF YOUR HEAD

Props: Three balls, two large knives.

This crazy routine fits well with a clown act. It requires very little juggling skill, but kids get a real kick out of it.

Juggler comes out on stage carrying a bag of props. He sets it down and introduces himself. "Hello, boys and girls. Do you know who I am?"

"No," they say.

"Why, I'm the great Dr. Dropo, world famous . . . ah . . . ah . . . let's see, I know I'm famous for something." He scratches his head. "Maybe if I look in my bag here, it will remind me what I'm famous for."

He holds up items and names them off. "Let's see, I have juggling

balls, juggling clubs . . . I can't figure this out. What's this?. . .
A book. What's it say, *HOW TO JUGGLE* . . . Hey that's it. I'm
Dr. Dropo, world famous juggler. . . what's juggling? Oh yes, I
remember it's throwing things up in the air and catching them—ah,
that's easy. Would you like me to do some juggling for you?"

"Yes," they say.

"OK, this will be a piece of cake . . . juggling—easy." He pulls
out three balls. "Do you want me to juggle them all with only one
hand or should I juggle them with my feet? Ah . . . let me try
it with two hands first, I don't want to do all the fancy stuff right
off."

He tosses all the balls up into the air, then screams and ducks as they
fall on top of him. "Hmm . . . let me try that again." He throws
them up again; this time he grabs for them but misses. They all come
down, hitting him. "OUCH-OUCH-OUCH! . . . Maybe this isn't so
easy after all."

He reaches into his prop bag and pulls out the juggling book and
reads for a few seconds. "Hmm . . . why I didn't know that . . .
Hmm . . . I see . . . yes . . . OK. Now I'll juggle these balls for
you." He picks up the balls and one by one tosses them up into
the air above his head where they fall, hitting him. "Ouch, ouch ,
ouch! . . . Hmm, maybe I need to try something a little easier
. . . like this." He holds up a single ball.

The juggler throws the ball up and tries to catch it with both hands,
but misses. He tries again, this time it hits him on top of his head.
Again he tries and the ball falls behind his back as he is running
forward to catch it. When he tries it again, he just barely manages
to catch it and hold on. He tosses it several more times and catches
it, gradually building up his confidence.

He becomes so confident now that he boasts, "I will now juggle this
ball with my eyes covered." He tosses the ball up and covers his
eyes with his hand. The other hand sticks out as if to grab the ball
as it falls, but the ball drops to the floor. "What . . . I missed? Let
me try that again." He tries it a second time but this time as he
covers his eyes with his hand he splits his fingers apart so he can
peek. He catches the ball and looks proud, even though the kids tell

him he peeked.

"One ball is pretty easy, let me try all three. I will now juggle all three of these balls." One by one he tosses up a ball, catches it, and puts it down. "Here's the red ball, now I'm juggling the blue ball, and finally I'm juggling the yellow ball . . . there, how was that, I juggled all three balls?"

The audience complains that he didn't do it right.

"Oh, you mean you want me to throw them up all at the same time and juggle them? OK, here goes." He throws them all at once and ducks so as not to get hit by the falling balls. "Hmm, that didn't work . . . maybe if I throw them one by one, I would get them going." He throws the balls up one by one wildly into the air and doesn't manage to catch any. "Hey, I think that's it; I almost had it that time. Let me try this again."

He tries throwing them again. This time he is able to juggle. He is overwhelmed with excitement and pleasure. "Hey! Look at this, I'm juggling! I don't believe it. I'm actually doing it. Wow, this is great. I've never done this before. Look at them go—up and down and up and down and up and down . . . There's only one problem . . . I don't know how to stop these things! I don't want to do this all day. HELP! Help me stop these crazy things." At this point one of the balls falls on top of his head and he drops the other two. "OUCH! Hey—that's it. When I want to stop I just hit myself in the head with one and then I drop them all."

Juggler reaches into his prop bag and pulls out two large knives. "Would you like to see me juggle these?"

"Yes," they shout.

Juggler looks with horror, "What!—are you crazy? I could get hurt doing that." He puts the knives back.

YOU TOO CAN BE A STUPID JUGGLER

Props: Six balls, small table or TV tray.

In this routine two jugglers are needed. One will play the part of a spectator, the other the juggler. The juggler will start off by performing some standard juggling movements and then move into the dialog below. The "J" stands for juggler, "A" is for audience, and "P" is for juggler's partner.

J: Have any of you ever tried to juggle? Easy isn't it?

A: (Various reactions.)

J: It's easy if you have someone that is a good juggler teach you. Really it's very easy to learn, it only looks hard. I'm not fooling, even an idiot can learn . . . how about you, sir, come up on stage. (Juggler motions to partner in the audience.)

P: No I can't, I'm too clumsy really.

J: (Juggler keeps motioning him to come up.) Come on.

P: No, I couldn't. I have a hard time even combing my hair in the morning. (He is bald.)

J: I see why. Come on up, the audience wants to see me teach you to juggle, don't you, audience?

A: Yeah. (He reluctantly comes up on stage, he looks clumsy.)

J: (Juggler hands him three non-bouncing balls. What's your name?

P: Wally Whipple.

J: Have you ever tried to juggle before, Wally?

P: No.

J: Well, by the time this show is over you will be juggling like a pro. Now take the balls in your hands like this and listen very closely to my instructions and make sure you follow them exactly as I explain them to you. You understand?

P: Yes.

J: OK, here we go. (Juggler now procedes to explain the cascade, but he talks very fast and with a lot of arm waving and makes it totally incomprehensible.) Take two balls in this hand and one in the other. You will toss the first ball, which is the one on your fingertips, up at a 78 degree angle with a vertical line that comes right down here. As the ball loses momentum, you release the ball in your other hand, pushing it up with the palm of your hand so it travels in an arc to the right. As the first ball comes down, quickly thrust your arm out to catch the ball while simultaneously tossing the third ball underneath ball number two. As you release the ball, flop your hand out to catch the second ball which will land in your right hand but remember to toss the other ball at the same time because the third ball is coming down.

At the same time toss ball number one back up into the air and catch ball number three before catching ball number two which is still in the air. But you must release ball number three before catching ball number two, before you can catch ball number one . . . You got it? Very easy, isn't it?

P: Ah . . . ?

J: OK, now let me see you try it.

P: All right. (He tosses all the balls up and makes a clumsy attempt at catching them and throwing them back up.)

J: No, no, didn't you listen to anything I said? Here, now try it again, but this time keep the balls off the floor. It saves you from bending over so much.

P: (He tries it again, the first two balls go all right, but the third hits him in the head.) OUCH!

J: You almost had it that time. Try it again.

P: I don't think I want to.

J: Why not?

P: I don't want to get hit by the ball again . . . it hurts.

J: Oh, pish-posh, it doesn't hurt. The people out there want to see you juggle, now come on.

P: All right. (He starts to juggle and third ball flies out sideways and hits juggler in the head.)

J: Ouch! (He rubs his head and looks at partner. Partner shrugs his shoulders in innocence.) OK, try it again. (This time the juggler stands on the other side of him. Wally begins to juggle, on the fourth toss the ball flies out of his hand and hits the juggler in the head.) Ouch! (He gives a suspicious look to his partner who again shrugs his shoulders.) Here, try it again. (The juggler stands behind him this time. Partner throws ball up and behind him. As the ball sails toward the juggler, he sees it and leaps away just, barely avoiding being hit.)

P: (Partner can't understand where the third ball went and looks around for it. He looks up, down, from side to side. Juggler comes around and hands him the ball.) How do you expect me to learn to juggle if you keep taking away my balls?

J: I'm not taking them away from you.

P: Then where did you get this?

J: Never mind, try it again. (This time the juggler holds up a small table or TV tray to use as a shield. Still his partner manages to toss a ball up over the shield and onto juggler's head.) That's it, that's enough, go back to your seat.

P: Hey, I'm just getting the hang of it now.

J: Well, hang it over there and sit down.

P: No, you don't, you promised to teach me how to juggle, now I want to learn.

J: OK . . . let's try some tricks. Let's see you do this. (He does the *knee bounce*. Wally is also able to do it. Juggler looks surprised but determined to discourage him.) All right, try this then. (Juggler does the *shower*, let's one bounce on the floor, catches it, and continues with the cascade.)

P: Let me see, how did that go? (He moves his arms in a circle trying to remember the pattern.) OK, here goes. (He is able to do it.)

J: Try this. (Juggler alternates between bouncing all three balls on the floor and the cascade.)

P: Ah, that looks simple. (He does it but adds a right *knee bounce* followed by a left *knee bounce* and ends up with a *foot tap*. Juggler looks at this with amazement and displeasure.) Hey, I've got one for you, can you do this? (He now does *columns* moving the odd ball from center to the left, then the right.)

J: Yeah! (Juggler does it too.) OK, wise guy, try this. (He does several *behind the back* tosses as he juggles.)

P: Ah, easy. (He does it.) OK, now watch this. (Wally cascades, then throws one ball up, and catches it on his arm with an *elbow catch*.) Can you do this one?

J: (Determined) Yeah, if you can do it, so can I. (He throws the ball up and reaches out to catch the descending ball. It comes down and smacks him in the forehead.) OUCH! . . . Let me try that again. (He tries it again, this time the balls misses his arm and falls on top of his foot.) OUCH! (He is frustrated and points to Wally's foot.) Oh goodness, look, your shoe is untied. (As Wally looks at his shoes, juggler picks up ball and sets it on his arm.) Ta-da! . . . I did it.

P: (Both of them are standing with a ball on their arms.) All right, do this one. (He snaps his arm up flinging the ball into the air where he grabs it and continues   juggling.)

J: Why, ah . . . sure. (He flips his arm up but the ball just flops to the ground.)

P: Are my tricks getting too hard for you? (Juggler gives him an evil eye.) Here, try this one all—

J: Nope, that's enough . . . go back down to your seat. This is my show, go find your own. Get . . . go on.

OOEY, GOOEY, AND BUZZY

Props: One small box.

This is a very easy routine requiring no juggling whatsoever. This has been a very successful routine with me for kids, and even adults get a kick out of it. Although this routine does not require any real juggling, it fits best following another juggling routine.

"Ladies and gentlemen, boys and girls, to demonstrate to you why I am world famous for my juggling powers, I will perform a very difficult trick for you.

"Most jugglers in order to show how skilled they are, juggle very large objects such as bowling balls, axes, and chain saws. Well, juggling that stuff is easy. Those things are so big that they're easy to catch and so they're easy to juggle. What's really hard to juggle are very small objects. Small objects are harder to catch and therefore harder to juggle. So I, Dr. Dropo, to show you my great juggling skill, will juggle for you some very small objects. I will attempt to juggle three, yes I said three, very teeny tiny mosquitoes. Yes, I said mosquitoes.

"I've been doing this trick for some time now and have used the same mosquitoes in all my shows. Consequently, we have become very close friends, in fact we are almost like family. I would like to introduce them to you."

Juggler pulls out a small box and opens it up. Poking his fingers inside he pulls out a very tiny mosquito, so small nobody can see it. Holding it between his thumb and first finger and wiggling them a little gives the appearance he has taken one of the tiny creatures out of the box.

"This one's name is Buzzy." He deposits the mosquito in his other hand and reaches into the box for another. "This one's name is Gooey." He takes out the third. "And this one's name is Ooey."

He holds them all in one hand. "Bow for the folks boys. OK, now for the three mosquito juggle." Juggler divides them up into each hand and starts to do the cascade, but just as he throws them, they all fly off. Frantically he jumps this way and that, trying to grab

them. "Hey! Where are you going? Get back here. We've got a show to give."

He grabs each of them and begins to juggle. "As I said, you are now about to witness mosquito juggling." The mosquitoes cooperate this time and the juggler begins tossing and catching the tiny creatures.

The juggler calls out names of tricks as he performs them. *"Under the leg, behind the back, floor bounce . . . juggling without looking."* He cocks his head sideways so as not to see, and continues to juggle without problem.

"With one hand." The other hand goes behind his back while one hand bobs up and down in front. "With the other hand." He switches hands. "With one foot and one hand." One hand goes behind his back while the other hand and one foot bob up and down. "Now the other foot and the other hand." He switches hands and feet. "Now both feet and both hands." He juggles with his hands and alternately lifts each leg up quickly, making a very funny appearance with all legs and arms swinging.

"I will now juggle them with just my little fingers." He sticks out his little fingers and begins to juggle. "This is called pinky juggling."

He bends his arms and sticks out his elbows. "This is called elbow juggling."

Bending forward he wiggles his nose back and forth. "This is nose juggling."

He grabs his little buddies and juggles normally again. "OK, boys let's pick it up a little and show the people some speed juggling." The juggler moves his arms very fast and lifts his feet up and down like pistons. Calling out names of tricks, the juggler performs them in fast motion.

"OK, Ooey do the *knee bounce*, Gooey do *behind the back*, Buzzy the *short floor bounce* . . . Hey, somebody is missing." Juggler stops with one mosquito in each hand and looks at them. "Where's Buzzy?" He lifts one hand to his ear as if to listen to what Gooey has to say. "On the floor?" He looks down but doesn't see anything. Stepping back one step he still doesn't see anything. Lifting up his foot he looks at his sole and makes an ugly face. "Ooooh!" The bottom of the shoe is wiped off on the floor.

"OK, boys and girls I will now show you the two mosquito juggle." He begins to juggle, then quickly slaps his neck. "Hey! . . . It's not lunch time yet." Pulling his hand away he looks down into his palm to see a crushed mosquito. "OH—OOEY! Ooey, I didn't mean to hit you so hard. Speak to me please." The juggler begins to cry. "Ooey, I'm sorry, sniff sniff, speak to me please, boo-hoo . . . What's that? . . . I think he's alive, and he's trying to say something." He turns to Gooey who is in the other hand. "Gooey, I think he's trying to say something to me."

The juggler brings Ooey up to his ear to listen. A smile creeps on to his face and with uncontrollable joy he exclaims, "He says he's OK!" and slaps his hands together in joy, accidentally crushing both of his little buddies. A sour look slowly creeps onto his face as he realizes what he has just done. Looking at his closed hands, he softly calls, "Ooey? . . . Gooey?" Opening up his hands slightly he peeks inside, sticks out his tongue, wipes his hands off on his shirt, and says, "Ooey-gooey."

JUGGLE-GUTS

Props: One large knife, three soft rubber hammers, two rubber balls, one boxing glove, three juggling scarves.

This is another simple routine requiring little juggling skill. The juggler brings a bag of props up on the stage with him. He starts by talking about jugglers who perform dangerous tricks.

"Audiences like to see jugglers put their lives on the line and juggle dangerous objects like knives, axes, chain saws, and the like. Those that juggle such objects have a lot of guts. I too have a bunch of guts, so I will jeopardize my life by bringing you a juggling demonstration you will never forget."

Juggler looks in his prop bag and pulls out a large deadly looking knife. He eyes it for a second and puts it back down. "Ladies and gentlemen, I will now put my life on the line and juggle three long and very sharp objects."

He reaches into his bag. "I will attempt to juggle for you . . ." He lifts up the knife as if referring to it and then puts it down. "I will attempt to juggle three long and very sharp . . . needles!" He holds up an empty hand but pretends to hold three sewing needles.

"Yes, these are three long and very sharp sewing needles." Juggler touches the tip of one with his fingers. "Ouch, yes they are very sharp . . . hey don't laugh, lady, I don't see you up here doing this. OK, ladies and gentlemen, here we go, this trick is known as needle juggling." Juggler moves arms as if he were actually juggling something.

Suddenly he stops, holds up three stiff fingers as if the needles were stuck in them. "Ooooo! . . . I keep catching the wrong end." He tugs on each finger as if pulling out the needles. The fingers are wiggled to show that the needles are now out. "Ah . . . that feels better, here we go again." He begins to move his arms in a juggling pattern.

As he juggles, he calls out the name of tricks and performs them. *"Under the arm, behind the back, under the leg* . . . OUCH!" He just stabbed himself in the rear end. "I knew I was going to get hurt with these."

"Let me try something that's not quite so sharp." He looks through his prop bag. "Here we go, I'll juggle these three hammers . . . that's pretty dangerous."

He proceeds to juggle but as he does, the hammers begin to hit him on the head. "Ouch-ow-ouch!" He stops juggling and rubs his sore head. "Let me try juggling something that's a little softer."

Juggler goes to his prop bag again. "Ah yes, here we go, a glove . . . a glove can't hurt anything. I'll juggle two nice soft round balls and this soft glove." He holds up the balls and a boxing glove.

"I won't get hurt this time." He throws them up and begins juggling. He performs a few tricks such as *under the leg, floor bounce, knee bounce,* and others.

"There I didn't get hurt that time." Just as he says that, the glove hits him across the head. "OW!" As he juggles it keeps hitting him. "Ouch-ouch-ouch! . . . That's it." He puts the balls and glove back.

"Let me find something else . . . something even softer." He looks around inside the bag. "Here we go . . . I will now demonstrate my unusual courage by juggling for you three large and deadly . . . scarves."

He pulls out the scarves and begins to juggle calling out the names of tricks he performs. The faster he moves, the funnier the movements become. Finally he steps on one of the scarves which has fallen on the floor. He slips on it and falls. With agonizing pain he slowly pulls himself up off the ground. "Ladies and gentlemen, forget it . . . I can't even juggle scarves without getting killed."

PLUNGERS AND DIRTY DISHES

Props: The juggler wears a white shirt and pants. Three dishes, three juggling clubs, and three short toilet plungers.

In this routine the juggler comes onto the stage without introduction or fanfare. He pulls out three juggling clubs without saying a word and begins to juggle. The white outfit is worn as an effect for the ending. An apron may be substituted for this outfit with similar effect.

Juggler stops and begins speaking to the audience. "I've always wanted to be a professional juggler. To get in front of an audience and perform brings real satisfaction. I used to juggle on street corners in Hollywood so that talent scouts would notice me and give me the big break I was looking for. I showed some real talent too by juggling various things like plates, bowling balls, and brooms. You name it, and I was out there trying to juggle it.

"Well, I got a break and landed my first job in show business and was offered a job working in a radio station. Unfortunately jugglers don't do too well over the radio. Anyway, you see, the owner of the radio station saw me juggling on the street one day. He came up to me and said I was just the person he had been looking for to work at his station. Well I went to work for him . . . he told me I was the best darn janitor they ever had at radio station KLUCK and I kind of felt like a kluck, sweeping up the place with three brooms. I decided then and there I wasn't going to juggle brooms any more.

"Well, you probably already guessed that I quit that job and went back out on the street corner. I was juggling these pins (juggling clubs) one day and this fellow comes up to me and says he likes the way I handle these things and offers me a job. He ran a local bowling ally. I thought it would be real exciting working there because he told me I would have a ball. Well, that job didn't last too long either. They kept me back behind the lanes all the time picking up these stupid pins and those heavy balls. I wasn't getting anywhere there, so I went back out on the street corner.

"I thought I found a new job with a little more class. I got a call from a school principal who told me I've got real class and he would like me to work for him. I was pleased and asked him what he liked about my act. He said I impressed him with how well I could handle plungers." Juggler juggles toilet plungers. "'Stop,' I said, 'that's enough.' I didn't take the job. I knew what that was going to lead to.

"I was out on the street corner again until just a few days ago when I got this job. It's not really what I wanted, but it's a living . . . Oh, I'm not part of the show. The main attraction hasn't shown up yet so I'm stalling for time. I see I've stalled enough so I'll get back into the kitchen and finish washing the plates." Juggler exits juggling plates.

BOUNCING BAGS

Props: Three pillows, three bean bags, one bouncing bean bag, one rubber ball, three axes, one carrot, trick magic wand which goes limp, and a large picture of three balls.

This routine uses someone from the audience. The performer will choose a likely candidate and have him come up on stage where he will be instructed in the fine art of juggling. The "volunteer" could perhaps be asked beforehand, be a member of the act, or be chosen at random from the audience.

The juggler begins the routine by showing several tricks. Various props can be used such as clubs, balls, rings, etc. The audience should be impressed by the fine juggling ability of the performer.

Juggler states, "Although the tricks I have been doing look very difficult, juggling is actually much easier then it appears. Anybody can learn. All it takes is the right teacher. You, sir, do you know how to juggle?"

"No," he answers.

"Would you come up here, please?"

Juggler continues, "To show you how easy it is to learn to juggle, I will teach—what's your name?

He says, "John Smith," or whatever his name happens to be.

"I will teach John here how to juggle. John, you say that you have never juggled before, is that right?"

He answers, "Right."

"Well, before this audience today I will teach you all you need to know to become a juggler. You can then go home and impress your friends with your new found skills. Are you ready?"

"Yes," he says.

"Juggling is very easy; it's just tossing and catching things like balls. Haven't you ever played catch with a baseball or football or something?"

"Yes." he replies.

"Then you have already juggled. The only difference between the juggling I do and what you have done is that I use three balls and you only one. Here take this ball in your left hand."

The juggler hands the ball to the spectator's right hand so that he reaches for it with his right hand instead of this left. As he reaches out with his right, juggler says the following. "No, I mean the other left hand . . . Gee wiz, a hundred people in the audience and I choose one with two left hands. Well, if I can teach you to juggle, then I can teach anyone. Now take this ball and toss it up and down . . . good."

"OK, now you're ready to learn three object juggling. By the way, John, are you by any chance a doctor?

He says, "No."

"I guess that doesn't matter, they never are." Juggler pulls out three axes. "Here, let's see you juggle these. Oh, I almost forgot. I want to make sure they're nice and sharp first."

Performer takes out a raw carrot and chops it with one of the axes to show how sharp it is. This is an old trick which is commonly used. The axes need not be sharp to chop the carrot. Hold the ax in one hand and hit the carrot quickly against the blade. Even a very dull blade will easily slice the carrot in this manner. The audience does not know this and believes the ax to be sharp.

"Now here, juggle these, but be careful that you don't cut yourself. The last volunteer I had was carried out on a stretcher . . . he was one of the lucky ones. Now you know why I asked if you were a doctor."

He is handed the axes. "OK, go ahead, start juggling." Spectator looks confused.

Before he does anything the juggler continues. "Well, what's wrong? Are you a little squeamish? . . . I see, Mr. Daredevil you ain't."

The axes are taken away from the spectator. "I have something more to your style." Juggler pulls out three pillows. "Here try these, you won't get hurt with them." Spectator tosses them around for a few seconds, which will bring some laughs.

"You're having a little trouble, I see. Maybe these pillows are too big . . . here try these." He is given three hand-sized bean bags. "OK, hot stuff, now juggle these." The spectator will struggle with the bean bags for a few seconds.

"OK, let's back up a bit, maybe I'm starting you out a little too fast, try two bags like this." Juggler throws each bag straight up and down one at a time. Spectator does the same. If he drops one, all the better, but most almost anyone should be able to do one at a time without too much trouble.

"OK, good, stay with two bags for awhile and let's try a trick."

The juggler has one regular bean bag and one bouncing bean bag. The bouncing bean bag is just a ball sewn inside a bean bag cover.

"Look at this." Each bag is tossed up and caught. The bouncing bean bag is then thrown onto the floor. It bounces back up and the juggler catches it. "Now you try it."

Spectator has two regular bean bags which don't bounce. He tries the trick but the bag falls dead on the floor.

Juggler asks, "What's wrong with you? Why didn't you bounce the bag?"

"I don't know," he says.

"Try it again, just like this." Juggler repeats the trick with the bouncing bag. Spectator tries the trick a second time and again his bag stays on the floor.

"What's wrong, why can't you get yours to bounce back? I'm beginning to think it's hopeless trying to teach you to juggle. It would take a miracle to get you to . . . hey, that's it, a miracle. I've got just the thing to give you the magic touch and make a juggler out of you."

The performer pulls out a magic wand. "Magic wands have special powers that will make even the most clumsy person an expert juggler . . . here, take this."

As the juggler hands the wand to the spectator the wand goes limp in his hand. "Hey, what did you do to my magic wand? Does this happen to everything you touch?" The wand is taken back and put away.

"Let me see . . . I must have something here, what with your abilities, you can manage to juggle. Oh, I found it. This is the only thing I have, I'm afraid, that you will be able to juggle."

He is handed a large picture of three balls. "Now take this picture and move it up and down, that's right, there you did it. Thank you. Everybody give him a big hand."

Instead of the picture the spectator could have been given three juggling scarves and allowed to try juggling them. Watching someone try to manipulate the slowly falling scarves can be hilarious.

THE WEENIE ZAMBINIS

Props: Two red juggling balls, one blue ball, one green ball, a stuffed hand, ridiculous looking hat, one golf ball, one blue bean bag or ball of clay the same color as the blue ball, three juggling rings.

This act involves a mischievous juggling ball named Clara. The concept of a disobedient prop has been around for quite some time. Here is my version of it.

The juggler runs out on stage and does a cartwheel or series of flips. The assistant throws three juggling rings out to him. He juggles them for a few seconds before handing them back to the assistant and then introduces himself.

"Let me introduce myself. I am Dr. Dropo, world famous juggler and acrobat. And this is my assistant, Dropette.

"As you know acrobats and gymnasts must be very flexible to perform all their stunts. To show you my great flexibility I will take my leg and wrap it around my neck."

The juggler reaches down grabs his leg and begins to pull it up slowly towards his neck. He struggles with it, grunting now and then. As he pulls it up, he twists his body so that his back is toward the audience. Candidly taking off his shoe he holds it up by his ear making it look as if he really did pull his foot up that far. The audience is not fooled however and laughs.

64

"For my next trick I will combine acrobatics and juggling. I will attempt a one-handed hand stand and while standing on one hand, I will juggle two balls with the other. OK, here I go."

The juggler bends down, places one hand on the ground, and then makes several short jumps trying to lift his feet up into a hand stand. On his last effort his feet go high up into the air but his arm collapses and he falls into a pile on the floor.

Looking towards his assistant he says, "Dropette, will you please give me a *hand* with this?" The assistant grabs the stuffed hand and gives it to the juggler. He looks to the audience and says, "As you see, one hand." He tosses it down on the floor, steps on it, and juggles two balls in one of his hands. "I am standing on one hand and juggling two balls."

"Now that's enough of my gymnastics, let me . . . who said 'Good'?" He looks out into the audience for the wise guy.

"Let me do some juggling for you now. Before I do, I would like to introduce to you three young jugglers and acrobats. I'm proud to have them in my act because I, Dr. Dropo, personally trained them. Before I have them come out on stage, I need to put on my juggling hat." He places a silly looking hat on his head with a blue bean bag hanging on it.

"I will now introduce to you the ZAMBINI SISTERS!" The juggler reaches into his prop box and pulls out a red ball. "This is Suzie Zambini . . . isn't she cute?" He reaches into the box and pulls out another red ball. "This is Sally Zambini." The juggler reaches back into the box and searches around. "And this is . . . and this is . . . Hey where's Clara?" The juggler looks all around.

"Have any of you seen Clara? She is a little blue ball about this big." His assistant tells Dropo that Clara is on his hat. "What? On my hat!" He takes the hat off and pulls Clara off. "What are you doing? Get off there and stop playing around; we have a show to give."

The juggler looks back at the audience. "I would also like to introduce to you the girl's little brother. This is Pee Wee." He holds up a golf ball. "He's too young and hasn't learned to juggle yet, but he plans on become a juggling ball when he grows up.

"Ever since I was a little boy I wanted to grow up and become a juggler, but my mother wanted me to be a brain surgeon. That's why I'm known as Doctor Dropo.

"Let me ask the girls what they would like to be when they grow up." Dropo takes one of the red balls in his right hand. "Suzie, have you ever thought of what you would like to be when you grow up?" The juggler moves the ball in an up and down motion as if it was nodding its head. "You have? Well, what would you like to be?" Juggler brings the ball up to his ear as if listening to it. "Oh, you would like to be a basketball, good.

"How about you, Sally, what would you like to be when you grow up?" He brings the other red ball up to his ear to listen. "A soccer ball, good.

"How about you Clara, what would you like to be?" He brings the blue bean bag up to his ear. "Good, you want to be President of the United States . . . WHAT! . . . President of the United States! . . . You can't be the President of the United States. The President is not a ball, and you're a ball and you have to stay a ball. Now, tell me really, what would you like to be?" The ball is bought to his ear again. "No, you can't be Lucille Ball either. Now seriously what would you like to be when you grow up?" Again he brings the ball to his ear. "That's just like you Clara . . . she wants to be a bouncer.

"Now let's show the folks some juggling. Oh wait a minute, I need to talk to you first, Clara. No goofing off this time you hear me. Last time we got on stage you started showing off and playing around and ruined the whole act and got us kicked off the stage . . . You're not going to be a bad girl this time are you?" As he says this he shakes his head and moves the bean bag back and forth as if it were shaking its head no.

"You're going to be a good girl, aren't you?" Juggler nods his head as he looks at Clara. The bean bag moves up and down in agreement. Dropo turns to the audience. "That's what I thought." As he is looking away, Clara begins shaking her head no. Dropo sees it out of the corner of his eye and turns to look at Clara with a frown. "CLARA!"

Clara quickly begins nodding her head again.

"OK, now let's show the people some juggling." Dropo juggles in the cascade pattern for a few seconds then stops. Let's do some tricks now. Say, let's do the *floor bounce.*" He begins to juggle. "Suzie, let's start with you, do the *floor bounce.*" The juggler tosses a red ball up in the air and lets it drop.

Catching it as it rebounds, he continues to juggle.

"Sally now it's your turn." The *floor bounce* is repeated.

"Clara you do the *floor bounce* now." The blue bean bag is tossed up into the air. When it comes down, it hits the floor and just lays there. Juggler looks surprised that it didn't bounce; he looks at the audience, then at Clara. "Clara, what are you doing? This is no time to be taking a nap."

He reaches down and picks up the bean bag and shakes it as if to wake it up. "Wake up . . . wake up.

"It's no use, she's fast asleep. I'll put her in my box until she wakes up." The bean bag is placed into the box and Dropo turns to go back to the center of the stage.

"What?" He looks back at the box as if Clara said something. "You're awake now?" He reaches in and makes a switch by pulling out a blue ball. "Are you sure you're wide awake, let's see." Ball is bounced on the floor. "OK, let's continue.

"Let's do another trick now. We'll do the *knee bounce.*" Juggler begins to juggle. "Suzie, do the knee bounce." Suzie does the *knee bounce.* "Sally, your turn, do the *knee bounce.*" Sally does the trick."

"All right, Clara it's your turn; do the *knee bounce.*" Clara is tossed into the air and the juggler's knee is lifted up for the bounce, but Clara goes to the other side of his body and does a *floor bounce.* "Hey . . . that's the *floor bounce* not the *knee bounce!*"

He listens to something she says. "Yeah, I know you missed the *floor bounce.* That's because you were asleep. We're doing the *knee bounce* now, let's try it again." This time Clara does an *elbow bounce.*

"Clara, what are yoooou doing?! That's not the *knee bounce*. Now quit goofing off and do the *knee bounce*."

As the juggler does the *knee bounce* with Clara, he hits the ball hard so that the ball flies high up into the air. The assistant honks a horn for sound effects. Juggler bends down on one knee and reaches out to catch the ball. "Clara! Why do you always have to make such a big production out of everything?"

Clara is causally dropped on the floor so that she rolls across the stage. "Clara, where do you think you're going? It's not time to go home yet . . . I don't care if you do have a date, get back here."

Dropo begins to juggle again. "The next trick will be . . ." Clara repeatedly is thrown high up in the air far above the other two as the juggler does the cascade. "Clara, what are you doing? Stop that, come down here right now." Clara joins the other two for a normal cascade.

"Now as I was saying before I was so rudely interrupted. My next trick . . ." Juggler begins to do *over the top* with Clara going back and forth over the other two. "Clara, stop that!"

The juggler grabs Clara and stops juggling. "If you don't stop fooling around I'm going to put you back into my box and keep you there for the rest of the show. What do you think of that?" Clara jumps from the juggler's hand and bounces off his head. "OUCH! Cut that out!" Juggler picks up the ball and begins the cascade again.

"As I was saying, my next trick will be . . ." Clara is continuously bounced on the floor, *simple floor bounce*. "Clara, you stop that!" Dropo grabs Clara. "That does it, next time you start horsing around I'm putting you back into the box and that's where you're going to stay. Do you understand me?" Clara nods her head yes. "Good."

"We will now do some bouncing tricks. We will do a combination of *elbow bounces* and *forearm bounces*." Juggler begins to juggle. "Suzie, you go first, do an *elbow bounce*" She does it. "Good, do another one . . . great. Sally, you do a *forearm bounce* . . . good. Now for a hard trick, Sally will do an *elbow bounce* followed by two *forearm bounces*. OK, go." Sally does the tricks.

"OK, Clara, your turn, do an *elbow bounce* . . . good. Now do a *forearm bounce.* " Clara hits the juggler on his head. "OUCH!" He looks stunned. "What's the big idea? . . . what do you mean, you slipped? . . . Oh, all right, try it again."

Dropo throws Clara up into the air, when she comes down she is caught between the juggler's biceps and forearm. He is surprised and looks at the audience then back at Clara.

"Clara, what are you doing? . . . Oh, you're tired so you're taking a break." Juggler cries out to Clara. "We're right in the middle of a show, you can't take a break now! Get back up there."

Clara is snapped back up into the air. "Now do the *forearm bounce.*" Clara does a combination *forearm bounce, elbow bounce,* and *knee bounce.* "That's enough."

Juggler goes back to the cascade. "Our next trick will be to—" Clara repeatedly bounces off the floor. "Clara, what are you doing! Now stop it. CLARA!" She now goes into continuous *under arm tosses.*

"Stop that Clara I'm warning you . . . OK, that does it, into the box you go. Now come here." Juggler does *Ferris wheel* and starts to walk briskly around the stage. "Oh, don't you try to run away from me. Come back here you."

Juggler does *behind the back toss.* "Don't you hide behind my back." He goes into alternating *under the leg tosses* using both legs. "Come out from under there. Hey! Stop that, cut it out. When I get my hands on you, you're going to be sorry."

Clara is tossed high into the air and when she comes down the juggler quickly grabs her and holds on tightly. "I've got you now. I'm going to stick you into that box for the rest of the show, what do you think of that?" Clara jumps from his hand and smacks him in the forehead. "OUCH! . . . Why you, come here."

Dropo chases the blue ball which has rolled out of sight behind a curtain. "I'm going to get you." The juggler follows after the ball. While he is out of sight of the audience, he picks up the ball and tosses it back out on stage. It is thrown so that it makes high bounces. The juggler then runs after it. "Stop you!" He catches up to the ball and grabs it. "Got ya!"

Juggler wiggles his arm as if Clara is putting up a struggle. "Oh no, you don't, you're not going to get away from me."

Clara springs from his hand into the cascade and then into columns. "Woops! Come back here." Juggler drops both red balls and leaps up and tackles her.

"I've got you now, and this time you're not getting away." Juggler wiggles the ball as if wrestling with her. "Oh no, you don't. I warned you, now you're going into that box." Juggler walks over to the prop box and tosses Clara in. "Now there . . . Oh stop your crying, I'm not going to let you out."

Juggler turns to audience. "As I was saying . . . what?" He looks toward Clara and walks to the box. "You say that you will now be a good girl . . . NO! I don't believe it . . . What do you mean pretty please? I said NO! . . . And stop that crying . . . What's that you say, if I don't let you out, you will hold your breath until you turn blue? . . . You're already blue! Now cut that out."

Juggler turns away then looks back. "What did you say? . . . You're really sorry for all the trouble you've caused and promise to be good for the rest of the show."

Juggler pulls her out of the box and says, "You promise to be a good girl if I let you out?" Clara nods, yes. "Oh all right then, let's continue."

Dropo turns to the audience. "For my final trick, I will bounce a ball on the floor, catch it with my foot, and then throw it back into the air where it will land in a perfect balance on my chin.

"All right, here we go." Juggler does the cascade. "Clara, why don't we start with you this time. Go ahead now." Clara hits juggler on top of his head. "OUCH! . . . That does it! . . . In the box with you."

Clara goes back into the box. A green ball is now pulled out. "Ladies and gentlemen, since Clara is no longer performing, her cousin Clarence will take her place in this final trick. This is Clarence

Zambini." He shows the green ball to the audience.

"OK, now for the trick." As he is juggling, Clarence begins to continuously bounce on the floor. "Clarence! What are you doing? That's not the right trick—stop it." Suzie and Sally now join Clarence so that all three are bouncing on the floor. "Suzie! Sally! Stop that, all of you!" The balls come back into the cascade.

"You kids better behave yourself, or I will put all of you in the box with Clara. OK, now are you ready for our final trick? Let's go. You first Clarence." Clarence hits the juggler on top of his head followed by Suzie and Sally. "OUCH-OUCH-OUCH! That's enough, you all go." Juggler grabs all three balls and puts them in the box.

SECTION TWO:
BALANCING

THE ART OF BALANCING

Balancing is a skill jugglers frequently use. The audience is filled with wonder and amazement at the sight of a performer balancing objects such as pool cues, tennis rackets, balls, plates, juggling clubs, swords, and other objects, often while juggling or manipulating other props.

Like juggling, balancing can be combined easily with comic patter and physical humor in an endless variety of ways. Professing to have the skill to balance objects, yet never able to do it quite like the "professional juggler," is the source of much amusement. The juggler, who portrays a clumsy show off, never manages to do the tricks right. He may perform some fine balancing tricks and movements, but appears to be out of control and looks like a goof. All of which makes the juggler a hilarious success.

Learning to balance simple objects is relatively easy and requires much less effort and coordination than ball or club juggling. For this reason many people prefer to learn balancing tricks and comedy.

BALANCING BASICS

There are different types of balancing but the type most frequently used by clowns and comic jugglers is referred to as vertical balancing.

Vertical balancing can be best described by using a long linear object such as a pool cue or a cane. I will use a cane in this explanation, but you can use almost anything of similar shape.

Stand a cane or some other linear object on end in the palm of your hand. Align the cane so that its center of gravity is directly above the balance point on your hand. If one end of the object you are using is heavier than the other (mop, baseball bat, tennis racket, pool cue), place the heaviest end up. That's right—up. To many people this sounds strange but an object with the center of gravity at the upper end moves more slowly if it begins to fall, so it is easier to correct and keep balanced. A three-foot-long cane, for example, balanced with the curved end at the top, is easier to control and keep erect than a three-foot dowel with a lower center of gravity.

If the support is stationary and there is no air movement, an object, once balanced, will reamain in balance. Air is seldom stagnant and the human body which is used as the support is never completely motionless. For these reasons the cane is continuously subjected to forces that may cause it to fall. The performer must constantly keep the object in balance by maneuvering the base of the cane so as to keep the balance point directly under its center of gravity.

The best way to accomplish this, and the real "trick" to balancing, is to fix your eyes to the top of the cane and keep them there. Don't look at your hand. The key to vertical balancing is detecting the slightest sway in the cane and correcting for it before the cane falls.

The biggest mistake beginners make when learning this type of balance is not watching the top of the cane. If the cane leans off balance, the first noticeable movement will be detectable at the very top. If you're constantly watching this point, you will be able to see the first sign of movement and will be able to correct it with the least amount

Figure 2-1

of effort. As you practice, you will develop a feel for the balance and will gain greater control, and the movement of the cane will become less perceptible.

Correcting the position of the cane is done by moving the hand forward, backward, left, right, or some combination these. Moving the entire body in the proper direction will accomplish the same thing. A common problem you may encounter is combining both body and arm movements, thus over compensating the correcting force and pushing the cane out of balance in the opposite direction.

What size object is best to balance? Try this. Take a pencil, stand it up vertically in the palm of your hand, and try keeping it in balance. You'll discover that the pencil is much more difficult to control than the cane was. The longer an object is, the easier it is to balance. A two-foot-long cane would have to lean twice as far from the vertical position as a four-foot cane would in order to be detected by the eye.

This is important in terms of showmanship. To most people longer objects look harder to balance. The performer will gain greater respect from an audience by balancing longer objects, even though less skill is required. Balancing an eight-foot pole on your hand or head looks impressive yet is much easier than trying to the do the same thing with a three-foot stick.

BALANCING TRICKS

Variations

Once you feel confident balancing the cane with your dominant hand, learn to do it with other parts of your body. First train the other hand, then try the top of your foot, a raised knee, an arm, your shoulder, finger, chin, nose, forehead, even your ear. One thing you must keep in mind with any of these positions is to place the cane where you will be able to see the top of it. You must be able to see the cane lean in order to correct it. That's why the vertical balance is virtually impossible to do from the top of the head.

When you are able to balance the cane on more than one hand, you can start tossing it from hand to hand, or from hand to foot, knee, or arm. When tossing a balanced cane or other object, keep it as vertical as you can and your eyes focused at the top. When you toss it from one place to another, don't physically throw it over, simply toss it straight up and exchange the base upon which it will balance. For example, if you have it in your right hand, gently toss it up a few inches, keeping it as vertical as possible. Move the right hand away and replace it with the left hand. The cane will come down on the left hand into a balance giving the appearance that it was actually thrown from one hand to the other. Try catching it in a similar manner with the knee, foot, and elbow.

Add some life to a simple balance by moving around. While holding the balanced object, step forward and backward, adjusting your hand as needed. Try sitting down on a chair or even on the floor, maintaining the balance the entire time.

Balancing Odd-Shaped Objects

So far I have referred only to linear objects, but objects with different shapes can also be balanced vertically by using the same principles. Things such as picture frames, chairs, suitcases, saxophones, small tables and even bicycles can be vertically balanced by standing them up diagonally or along their longest axis, heavy end up.

BALANCING ROUTINES

KNIVES SCARVES & SNAKES

Props: One large knife or machete, three juggling scarves, one peacock feather, three battery operated electric shavers.

This is a simple routine but full of laughs. It requires the aid of a youthful member of the audience. The only real juggling in the entire routine are the few tricks done at the start.

Juggler comes out on the stage juggling three balls. One by one he calls out the trick he is about to perform then does it. Several tricks are performed.

"Ladies and gentlemen, boys and girls, the juggling tricks I am about to show you now employ some unusual items and are extremely dangerous. Because of the great danger involved with these tricks I must caution you, don't attempt them at home, show them at work or at school instead, because your family and friends will think you're crazy. . . No, just kidding. The tricks I am about to demonstrate for you are very dangerous and if you do try them at home please make sure a doctor is present.

"I need to warn you that if the sight of blood frightens you, feel free to leave now. I never know from one day to the next how these tricks will turn out.

"Before I begin I will need an assistant. You, please, would you come up here?"

A boy comes up on stage. "What's your name?"

"Bill," he says (or whatever his name may be).

"OK, Bill, I'm going to have you help me with some balancing tricks."

Juggler pulls out a large machete and hands it to the boy. "Here, hold this please.

"To start out with, I will put my life on the line and perform for you some amazing feats of balancing. I will attempt to balance one very large and very sharp . . . feather."

Juggler pulls out a peacock feather and balances it on his hand. From there the feather is moved up and balanced on his nose. A peacock feather is used because it can be balanced with no prior practice or preparation.

After demonstrating a few balancing tricks the juggler continues. "OK, Bill, hand me the machete."

Bill gives it to him. Juggler hands the feather to Bill. "Before I go any farther, I want you to try to balance this feather on your hand to see how much coordination you have."

The boy should be able to balance it easily.

"OK, good. Now the audience wants to see something really dangerous such as balancing this razor-sharp machete."

The juggler motions with it as if he were going to balance it on his nose. He looks to the audience. "If a slip-up occurs and you see lots of blood, don't panic; it's happened many times before and I am still alive and healthy."

He turns to the boy, hands him the machete. "Here balance this machete on your tongue."

He waits for response, then turns to audience. "You didn't expect ME to try that trick did you? That's why I'm still alive and healthy."

Juggler puts feather and machete away. He thanks the boy and sends him to his seat.

"The types of things jugglers juggle nowadays are getting more bizarre. You've probably seen jugglers juggle chain saws. Well, I am now going to show you my version of chain saw juggling . . . Quiet, please . . . I must have silence as I fire up my engines."

Juggler takes out three battery operated electric shavers and turns them on. "I'm still a beginner and haven't worked up to full-sized chain saws yet. But you know, I have a friend who can juggle them . . . we call him lefty.

"Now, what you've all been waiting for . . . snake juggling. That's right, snake juggling, the tossing and catching of live poisonous cobras. This type of juggling originated in India and in India they do it with live cobras. But we're not in India, and I couldn't find any cobras, and besides I'm chicken, so I will use scarves. You can use snakes when you try it at home if you want to."

Juggler now takes three scarves and juggles them. This can be very funny by doing every variation and trick the juggler can think of. Many unusual tricks can be performed with scarves because they float down giving plenty of time to be caught.

Instead of using scarves, the juggler could have juggled rubber snakes or rubber chickens. Rubber chickens, which are available at magic shops, can be stiffened by inserting a wooden dowel inside them. Prepared in this way, these chickens can be balanced or juggled like ordinary juggling clubs, creating lots of laughs.

CHICKEN BALANCING

Props: One sword and sheath and a rubber chicken with a wooden dowel inserted inside to stiffen it so it can be balanced on end.

This is a very easy routine requiring only simple balancing skill.

The juggler claims to be able to balance a large deadly looking sword. He takes a sword and sheath. Grabbing the handle of the sword, he pulls the blade halfway out of the sheath and says, "Would you like to see me balance this on my nose?"

"Yes," they say.

He pulls the sword all the way out and throws it down. Taking the sheath he begins to balance it on his nose. He looks at the audience, "You didn't think I was crazy enough to use the sword did you?"

"Yes," they say.

"Well—I'm not one to disappoint my audience. I'll try to balance the sword on my hand and my chin for you."

He picks the sword up. "I don't mind trying this," he says with confidence. "This sword isn't sharp anyways—see." He grabs the blade with one hand and pulls with the other end. "YAAAH!" A look of agony races across his face. He holds his hand as if he just sliced it open. "Who sharpened this stupid thing? . . . must have been somebody who saw my last act.

You don't expect me to balance it now do you? I might cut something," he says as he rubs his neck and wiggles his fingers. Juggler makes pleading face hoping audience will let him off the hook.

"All right, all right, I'll do it for you. Nobody will be able to say I'm a chicken juggler—a turkey maybe, but not a chicken.

He takes a big gulp and fearfully stands the sword up on his hand. It loses balance and falls towards him "YIKES!" He screams and jumps to the side allowing it to slide past him and onto the floor. Breathing hard and with tongue sticking out he says, "Gee that was a close one."

Reluctantly he picks the sword back up and attempts to balance it again. As he holds it again, it starts to lean towards him. The juggler desperately tries to keep it from falling over by blowing vigorously on it. The sword straightens back up and he looks relieved but again it starts to lean towards him he again blows with all his might to rebalance the sword. It straightens back up, he re'axes. But again it starts to fall, he blows but it keeps coming. He gives it a big long blow using all his might and sound effects. The sword falls, hitting him on the forehead with the handle. "Ouch!"

The juggler looks toward the audience, "Are you sure you want me to do this?" They do.

He stands the sword up on his hand, but it begins to lean one way then another. He walks around trying to keep it upright. As he moves around, he stumbles, tossing the sword end-over-end up into the air. Desperately he reaches up to save it. As it comes down he catches it between his arm and chest pretending to have been stabbed.

"Ohhh! It got me." He staggers around making a ridiculous production out of the affair. Looking at the audience with a silly grin he says, "Just kidding . . . Listen I don't care if you do call me a chicken juggler I would much rather be called that then called dead." He quickly pulls out a rubber chicken, stiffened with a wooden dowel, and balances that on his chin.

THE DANCING CANE

Props: One cane with a curved handle.

This routine involves the use of a controlled loss of balance and relies heavily on physical comedy—body movement and facial expression.

A skilled juggler first demonstrates a few balancing tricks without flaw. A second juggler, who is far less skillful, attempts to imitate the tricks performed by the first.

"That was nothing, wait until you see this," he says. The juggler picks up the cane and holds it vertically at arm's length, giving it a good looking over. "I will now amaze you with my balancing skills. I will first balance this cane on one finger."

The juggler holds the cane vertically as if to place it on his finger that way. He sticks his finger out and rather than balancing the cane on top of the finger he hooks the Handle on it and lets the cane hang. "TA-da." Nobody is impressed.

"What's wrong? Nobody's applauding, aren't you impressed?"

Some may answer "No."

"OK, then watch this." He turns it sideways and balances it horizontally across on of his fingers. "Ta-da."

There's little response from the audience. "What's a matter? Haven't you ever seen a balancing act before? . . . OK, I'll do it the hard way."

Still holding the stick horizontally he lifts one leg off the ground. "This is called the double balance."

He puts his foot back down. "OK now I'm ready for the tough stuff." Gently he places the cane vertically on top of his hand, but it falls, hitting him on his head. "Ouch!" He screams. Rubs his head and tries it again.

Attempting to balance it again, it falls smacking him on his head. "Ooow!—stop that. Take this you!" Holding the cane firmly he swings it downward hitting his leg to teach the uncooperative stick a lesson, "Ouch!" Grabbing his injured leg he hobbles around for a few of steps.

"Let me try again." He places the cane into a vertical balance on his hand. "Hey, it worked," he says with surprise.

The cane now begins to lean. Quickly he tries to straighten it out. The cane leans to one side then to the other. The harder the juggler tries, the more the cane wabbles. Soon he is running all around making an attempt to maintain the balance. Running in circles, wobbling the cane back and forth, he stumbles and loses the cane only to accidentally catch it in the other hand or on his foot or elbow. He looks surprised but continues to struggle to maintain the balance.

His struggling can take on the appearance of a dance running and twisting, this way and that and contorting the body in humorous positions. The tricks can vary as much as the skill of the juggler will allow. The cane leans towards the audience ready to fall on top of those in the front row, but never leaving the juggler's hand.

Finally the juggler trips, tossing the cane into a spin in the air, and as it comes down it hits the juggler on top of his head. "Ouch!" he screams and staggers around the stage in a daze before making a comedy fall.

WOODY TOOTI

Props: One large juggling ring and a wooden dowel or stick for balancing.

The juggler enters carrying or balancing the stick in his hand. He introduces himself and then introduces his unusual balancing stick. "This is my pet stick, Woody Tooti." Extending the end of the stick to someone in the audience he says, "Here would you like to pet him? . . . What's the matter, haven't you ever seen a stick before?

"This is no ordinary stick mind you, this is a very special stick who is highly trained. Let me show you . . . Woody, stand up, come on, that a boy."

The Juggler balances the stick on top of his hand. "OK, Woody, play dead." The stick falls over and drops to the floor. "See what I mean, he follows my every command. But that's not all he can do—watch this. Woody, lie down."

The stick is balanced horizontally across the juggler's first finger. "Good, now roll over." The stick is twirled between the fingers so that it rolls over. "That-a-boy."

The juggler continues, "My trained stick can also balance on my ear." The stick is placed horizontally between the juggler's ear and the side of his head like a huge pencil.

"Oh this is a very talented stick, he can jump too. Show the folks Woody." The stick is tossed directly up a couple of inches and caught remaining balanced. The juggler looks at the stick and says, "That was nice but let's jump higher this time Woody, that little jump you made wasn't very impressive."

The juggler listens to something the stick says. "What do you mean you're afraid of heights? How can a stick be afraid of heights? Sticks are made from trees and trees grow to enormous heights . . . what's that . . . I don't care if you were just a little pygmy pine—now jump."

The juggler moves his hand up and down as if to toss the stick up, but he does it just slowly enough so that the stick does not leave his hand, making it appear as though the stick is clinging tightly to his hand.

"Hey, what's the big idea? You didn't jump—you didn't even lift your feet off my hand . . . I don't care if you're afraid of heights, we have a show to give. This time you had better jump." The juggler tosses the stick up and lets it come straight down unable to catch it, the stick lands on top of his foot.

"YOOOOW! Ouch ouch, you clumsy oaf what's the big idea? . . . What do you mean you didn't know where I was . . . well open your eyes numbskull, it's not that scary up there. Look I'm just as high up as you are and I'm not afraid. Keep your eyes open and let's try it again."

The juggler stands with the stick balanced in the palm of his hand. "OK Woody—jump!"

The stick stays on the juggler's hand but leans over falling onto the juggler's forehead as if trying to grab onto something to keep from falling. "Would you let go of me—get back up there."

The stick is pushed back up into a balance but immediately falls back down towards the juggler's head. "Get up there." He quickly sets the stick back up, but it falls again. "Get up there I said."

Woody falls again. "Let go—stop it!" Finally, it falls and rests against the juggler's forehead. The juggler is exasperated and just stands there looking stupid.

"Would you let go of me? . . . Now stop fooling around. You jump or I'll sell you to a toothpick factory, now get up there."

The stick is balanced again on the juggler's hand. "Ready, one, two three—jump!" The stick jumps up into the air turns halfway and hits the juggler on top of his head. "OUCH! . . . Why you—I have a good mind to ring your skinny little neck, what do you think about that?"

As he looks at the stick, it responds by slapping him across the side of his head—WHACK!

"Ooow! . . . Oh you've asked for it, I'm going to ring your neck." The juggler pulls out a juggling ring, places it on the stick, and spins it around. As the ring is being swung, the juggler makes a noise like a turkey gobbling or some other ridiculous sound. He spins the ring for a few seconds then removes it. The stick continues swing as if it were dizzy.

"OK trouble maker what did you think of that?" The stick starts beating the juggler on top of his head and back. The juggler ducks and runs around trying to get away. The stick follows continuing to beat the back of the the juggler's head and shoulders.

"Ow, stop it—ow ow, stop it—ow ow ow! Woody, you little rat, cut it out—ow!"

The stick stops and the juggler reaches over to grab it with his other hand. As he does so, the stick smacks it, "OUCH! Why you—"

He grabs again and it hits him again. He tries a couple more times getting hit each time.

Finally he grabs hold of the stick. The stick wiggles furiously to escape but can't. The angry juggler bites the stick. "Take that."

The stick slips out of one of the juggler's hands. "Come back here."

The juggler tries to grab the end of the stick but it runs away. The juggler chases after it. The stick bites the juggler's lower leg and holds on tight. Juggler yells, "Ooow—let go, stop biting my leg." He tries to kick the stick free but it continues to hold on like a little bulldog. Finally the juggler manages to kick the stick free. The stick then grabs a bite of the clown's rear end and holds on.

"Yow!" The juggler runs off the stage kicking his legs high and holding tightly onto the stick.

HECKLE AND JUGGLE

Props: Two eggs, one stick for balancing, and a set of juggling balls or clubs.

This is a comedy routine for two, the performer and a planted heckler. It is an adaptation of a routine by Frank Lane.

The performer is billed as an accomplished juggler. Heckler sits with the audience. Juggler is "J" and Heckler is "H". Music is played as the juggler enters the stage juggling (this is the only juggling in the routine).

J: Ladies and gentlemen, I will now amuse you with a few clever balancing tricks. (Juggler does two or three elementary tricks.)
H: Hisss . . . Boo! (Juggler stops for a second, lifts his eyebrows as if wondering where the noise came from, then he continues with another simple trick. This time he drops the stick.)
H: Boo! Boooo! (Juggler looks around at the audience and appears annoyed.)
J: Did I hear something?
H: Yeah . . . Boo!

J: What do you want?

H: I want to know what's going on behind that curtain?

J: (Very annoyed.) Why, nothing is going on behind that curtain.

H: Nothing is going on in front of it either.

J: Oh, a wise guy, Uh? I'll have you understand my father gave me over a thousand dollars so I could learn to juggle and balance.

H: What did you do with the money?

J: Will you mind your own business? Shut up and let me do my juggling act.

H: Are you going to do any juggling?

J: Yes, I am.

H: Well, so long. (Heckler gets up and starts to walk out, then stops and faces the stage.) You ought to be ashamed of yourself.

J: Me? You look like a pan-handler.

H: Can I help it if I work in a hospital?

J: Say, that's a pretty tie you have on.

H: Yes, it was given to me by my fairy godfather.

J: By your who?

H: My fairy godfather. Haven't you got a fairy godfather?

J: No, but (laugh) I've got an uncle I'm not quite so sure of.

H: Well, I'm not so sure of you either.

J: (Smile disappears from juggler's face and he appears to be sore again.) Oh, let me alone. If you don't like the show, go get your money back.

H: (Disgusted.) That's what's so bad. I had a free pass.

J: I'm sorry ladies and gentlemen for the interruption . . . I shall proceed to do some more tricks, intermingled with funny and witty sayings to amuse you. I will now—

H: Hey . . . do you know the difference between a bathroom and a dining room?

J: (Not caring to answer.) The difference? No, I don't know.

H: (Laughs aloud.) Well, you ain't coming over to my house.

J: Ladies and gentlemen, I'm going to show you one of the finest balancing tricks that man has ever invented. In this trick I shall

H: Hey! Your laundry just came back.

J: I beg your pardon?

H: I said your laundry just came back.

J: (Trying to ignore him.) Oh, that's fine.

H: Yes, they refused it.

J: (Exasperated.) Listen, will you go home?

H: I would, but I haven't got the car fare.

J: If I give you the car fare, will you go home?

H: Sure I will.

J: Where do you live. (Juggler puts his hand into his pocket to pull out some money.)

H: Italy.

J: (His hand comes out and he looks disgusted.) Listen, you're a pretty smart fellow. I'll tell you what I'll do. I'll show you a trick close up. Come on up here.

H: You mean you'll let me stand right next to you as you do your juggling tricks?

J: That's exactly what I mean.

H: Well, I don't know (hesitatingly). But I'll try anything once. (He goes up on stage. He appears awkward and embarrassed.)

J: Now, feller, you just watch me and I think you'll appreciate the difficulty of these tricks. (Juggler does a good trick, bows and the audience applauds. Heckler stands there looking back toward the wings, maybe thinking he'll see a girl in tights or something. Juggler jerks him around.) Never mind the girls. What did you think of that trick?

H: (Sneeringly.) Huh, my boy has showed me that trick before.

J: (Astounded.) What? You mean to stand there and tell me your kid knows how to juggle and he showed you this trick?

H: Sure, I got a clever kid.

J: (Appealing to audience.) Can you imagine that, ladies and gentlemen, here I do one of my best stunts, an original trick, and this man says his kid already thought the trick up and showed it to him.

H: Yes, that's right, my son showed me. He can do lots of things.

J: Oh I see, he's a regular genius. (Heckler nods in agreement.) Does your son do any magic?

H: Oh, you bet he does, He could make you look like a rank amateur.

J: He would? My, he must be good. Do you mind if I showed you a little magic trick?

H: No, that's all right. Go ahead; you won't disturb me.

J: I think you'll really enjoy this one. (Heckler is wearing a sport coat with pockets on the side.) Let me see, I will have to use your coat, do you mind? (Juggler examines coat.)

H: No, go right ahead. (Coat remains on Heckler.)

J: You say you son is an expert magician? (Juggler is getting more confident now, as he is going to put one over on this wise guy.)

H: Yes, my son can do most any magic trick. (He is beginning to lose his confidence because he doesn't know what's coming.)

J: That's fine, now first we take this egg, break it, and put it into your right coat pocket. (Juggler takes an egg and breaks it open. Lifting up the heckler's arm he drops the egg into his right coat pocket.)

H: Hey, what's the idea? (He tries to pull the coat away, but the juggler keeps hold of it.)

J: It's all right, my friend, it's just part of this wonderful trick.

H: (He gives a silly laugh.) Oh, I thought you was going to spoil my coat.

J: Now the second thing . . . you understand there are two parts to this trick. We are now on the first part. The second half of the first part is to break another egg, like this, and then drop it into your left coat pocket. Now we have one broken egg in each of your pockets.

H: (Heckler appears ready to sink through the floor.)

J: You say your son is a fine magician, uh?

H: (He is not so confident now.) Yeah, my son showed me some good tricks . . . I think it was my son.

J: Friend, as I told you before, there are two parts to this trick. The first part is to break the eggs and put them in your pocket. The second part is to make the eggs disappear. Now I did the first part all right, but I tell you truthfully, I don't know how to do the second part. You see I'm a juggler, not a magician, and I don't have the faintest idea how to get rid of them.

H: What am I going to do? (He sticks his hands into his pockets and pulls them out dripping eggs and makes a sour face.)

J: That's very simple. You go right home, and perhaps your son will show you how to make those eggs disappear. (Juggler takes him by the arm, walks him to the edge of the stage. The audience is laughing and he is ushered off the stage. Juggler returns to the center of the stage wiping his hands and continues with the rest of his show.)

SECTION THREE:
CIGAR BOXES

CIGAR BOX MANIPULATION

Cigar box manipulation has been used by jugglers and clowns for many years to please and delight audiences. Many jugglers like to incorporate skills in cigar box manipulation into their shows because it provides an interesting and entertaining departure from the more typical ball and club juggling.

Cigar box manipulation was introduced to the world in the 19th century by Japanese jugglers, who at the time used solid wooden blocks. American and European jugglers copied this unique form of juggling, replacing the heavy wooden blocks with empty cigar boxes. Today real cigar boxes are rarely used. Specially made wooden boxes are now the standard. Although some jugglers still use genuine cigar boxes, hollow wooden boxes are most popular because they can withstand the heavy physical abuse received during practice.

What is cigar box manipulation and how is it done? Basically, it is balancing, moving, and tossing cigar box-sized boxes without dropping them on the ground. Unlike ordinary juggling where the props are continuously tossed in the air, cigar boxes are manipulated. The juggler starts off by holding the boxes in what is known as the *home position* as illustrated in Figure 3-1. The boxes are then

Figure 3-1

rearranged without letting any of them hit the floor. As you see from the figure, slightly separating the boxes will cause the center box to drop. A skilled manipulator can move any box from one position to another, have it spin, flip, and balance without dropping any of them. This may sound easy at first, but try it and see. You will find even the simple tricks described here are extremely difficult until you learn the secret behind it.

CIGAR BOX TRICKS & MOVEMENTS

End-Turns

The first manipulation you should master is the end-turn. It is the simplest cigar box movement, much like the cascade is to juggling. To begin, line up the boxes end to end in front of you at about waist height, this is called the *home position*, see Figure 3-1. The letters on the boxes are used to aid you in following the movement of the boxes.

Hold the boxes together tightly so the center box does not slide out between the two outside boxes. Take box C and quickly move it away from the center box and turn it upside down, trapping the center

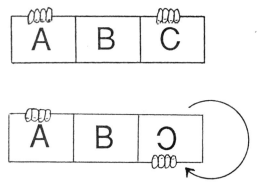

Figure 3-2

93

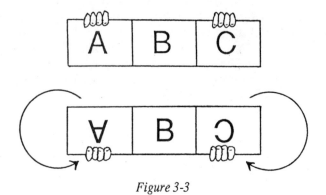

Figure 3-3

box before it falls (Figure 3-2). The first time you try this you are likely to find the center box lying on the floor with you scratching your head wondering what went wrong.

Pick it up and try again with one added movement. This time lift up slightly on all three boxes as you begin the maneuver. This upward movement need not be more than a few inches and if done correctly will be unnoticable to most observers. This trick provides momentum to the center box which causes it to hang in the air long enough for you to complete the rotation of box C. This upward motion is *very important* and is used for all cigar box movements.

Now reverse the movement by turning box C back upright, again starting with a slight upward swing. You should now be back in the home position.

Practice end-turns with each hand. Once you can do this maneuver with either hand, combine them by turning both ends at the same time (Figure 3-3). Reverse the movements to return to the home position.

Spins

Now let's learn how to spin the center box. Lift all boxes up as if to do an end-turn but this time at the peak of the lift, let go of

94

the center box. As box B is released give it a counterclockwise spin, see Figure 3-4. Spins can be half a turn, full turn, or just about any number of revolutions you care to tackle.

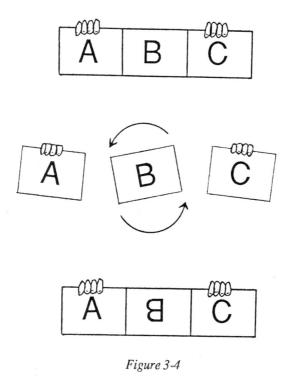

Figure 3-4

Take-Outs

One of the most impressive cigar box moves is to release an end box, grab the center box, swing it down and around and clamp the end box in the center position, see Figure 3-5 on the next page. This movement requires a little more speed than those discussed so far. Practice doing this with each hand.

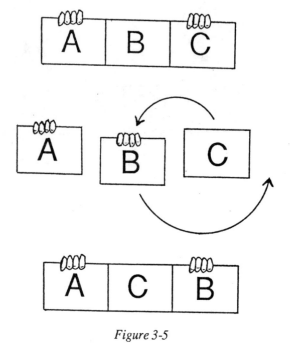

Figure 3-5

Crossed Hands

In this movement both hands are released from the end boxes and crossed over to grab opposite boxes (Figure 3-6). Swing boxes up, at top of swing quickly release both hands, cross arms grabbing box A with the left hand and box C with the right hand.

After practicing all these moves, try mixing them and combining two or more together. Use your imagination and develop movements on your own. The number of movements you can come up with is limitless.

Figure 3-6

Hinged Cigar Boxes

The cigar box tricks described so far require some degree of skill. By using a set of specially prepared hinged cigar boxes, the juggler, regardless of his abilities, can fool the audience into believing he has great skill.

Hinged cigar boxes consist of a set of three boxes joined at the corners, see Figure 3-7. When held together, they look like any other ordinary set of cigar boxes used by jugglers. But because they are attached, several seemingly difficult tricks can be performed with ease. A few of these tricks are described below.

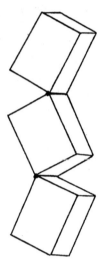

Figure 3-7

Start from the home position, with both hands holding the top of the end boxes. The first movement is to release one hand and grab the box from below (Figure 3-8). This should be done with a slight upward swing of all the boxes, just as if you were doing any other cigar box movement. This movement will reinforce your deception. This simple trick can be performed with either hand and can be done in reverse as well.

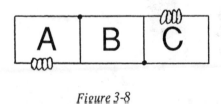

Figure 3-8

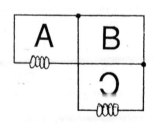

Figure 3-9

98

With the hands positioned as in Figure 3-8 an *angle balance* is obtained by swinging box C down under box B (Figure 3-9).

A *side-to-side balance* is achieved by simply putting box A on top of box B (Figure 3-10). The juggler uses only one hand to maintain this balance.

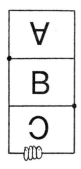

Figure 3-10

An impressive *end-to-end balance* can now be easily performed by gently tossing boxes A and B up while rotating box C (Figure 3-11).

Equally as impressive is to reverse this movement and come back into the *side-to-side balance*. Many balancing tricks can be performed while the boxes are stacked in an *end-to-end* or a *side-to-side balance*. The stack, for example, can be balanced on the palm of the hand, on the elbow, knee, or chin.

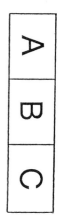

Figure 3-11

CIGAR BOX ROUTINES

THE INCREDIBLE CIGAR BOX ROUTINE

Props: Three normal cigar boxes and one set of matching hinged cigar boxes.

This routine has no dialog, relying entirely on the juggler's movements and facial expressions.

The juggler picks up three normal cigar boxes and places them, one at a time, in an *end-to-end balance*. Pushing them up from the bottom with force, he sends two of the boxes flying into the air. He grabs one in his free hand and clamps the third between the other two. He continues by doing a few simple cigar box movements such as *end turns*.

He now swings the center box up into the air and hits it hard with one of the end boxes. This sends it flying sideways to the edge of the stage. He throws up one of the other boxes. As it is in the air he hits it too, sending it out with the first box. Looking at the remaining box he tosses it underhanded towards the other two.

He picks up three new cigar boxes—hinged cigar boxes that look just like the first set. He pretends that they are just like the other ones. Juggler faces the audience while holding the boxes in the home position.

The first trick he does is to jump up over them with both feet bringing the boxes around behind his back. He then jumps back so that the boxes are in front of him again.

His second trick, one which appears very difficult, is to toss the boxes into a *side-to-side balance*. He then tosses them back into an *end-to-end balance*. Pausing, he gestures for audience to applaud.

While the boxes are in and *end-to-end balance* he performs various balancing tricks. Some tricks may include, balancing on his head, knee, elbow, or chin. He now swings the boxes down into a *side-to-side balance*. He signals for the audience to applaud. As they are applauding, he bends over to bow. Accidentally while he is bowing the boxes slip and dangle to reveal the gag. Juggler looks embarrassed.

STICKY BOXES

Props: One set of hinged cigar boxes.

This routine works well for clowns and can be performed almost anywhere.

"I will now do a trick which defies all description. I will razzle-dazzle you with my lighting quick reflexes and blinding speed. I will take these ordinary cigar boxes and manipulate them in a manner rarely seen by man or beast.

"I'm proud of this trick because I've had the pleasure of performing it before president Reagan . . . was elected."

The juggler takes the boxes in the home position. He swings them up all together slightly and grabs right hand box on end, see Figure 3-8 The boxes will come apart slightly giving the appearance that they are separated. He now swings the lift hand box down and under the middle box (Figure 3-9). Again he lets the boxes come apart slightly. Box A is raised onto box B to form a *side-to-side balance* (Figure 3-10). Now the juggler does what appears to be a very difficult trick. He throws the boxes into an *end-to-end balance*. "Ta-da."

He continues, "Now to show you some superb balancing." Juggler balances stacked boxes on his hand. He encourages the audience to give him some applause. He then moves the boxes onto his elbow and balances them. Again he signals the audience to give him some applause. As they are applauding, the boxes lose balance and fall, whacking juggler on his head. "Ouch!" He says as he grabs his head and reaches for the falling boxes. He holds them upside down, boxes sticking together at the hinges, exposing the trick.

CIGAR BOX MADNESS

Props: Three cigar boxes and a set of hinged cigar boxes.

This is a cigar box routine requiring only basic cigar box manipulative skills. A female assistant is required. She uses the hinged cigar boxes to perform what looks like very difficult cigar box tricks. This routine fits well following a typical juggling routine. The "D" stands for Dr. Dropo and "A" for assistant.

D: Jugglers have many skills and amazing physical abilities. I will now perform for you what is known as cigar box manipulation.

At the turn of the century real cigar boxes were used, but I use solid wooden blocks. (The cigar boxes are not really solid wood but ordinary hollow juggler type cigar boxes. Two of the boxes are tapped against each other to show they are solid.) Witness some of the amazing feats of skill in maneuvering these blocks without dropping them, (Performer now does a few simple cigar box movements. Finally the juggler attempts to move the box on the left to catch the center box so as to end up like Figure 3-9. Box A, however, slips off. He tries it again still without success.)

A: (As Dr. Dropo is attempting this trick, his assistant picks up a set of hinged cigar boxes.) Hey, Dropo . . . is this what you're trying to do? (She takes the boxes and effortlessly performs the trick.)

D: (Dropo has a stunned look on his face.) Why . . . yes, let me try it again.

A: Dropo, can you do this? (She now throws the boxes up into an *end-to-end balance.*)

D: (Dropo is surprised at what he's seen but acts as if the trick was elementary.) Why if you, an ordinary assistant, can do it then I, the great Dr. Dropo, can surely do it. (He tosses the boxes up and way out to the right so that they fly several feet away and land on the ground. He looks puzzled.) Let me try that again. (He attempts it a second time. This time the boxes go straight up into the air over his head. When they come down Dropo ducks but is hit by them.) Ouch! Ouch! . . . I'll get it this time. (He picks them up to try again. The boxes are tossed straight up over his head again, but as they come down he ducks and jumps out of the way. He looks totally confused. Suddenly an idea hits him and he points out into the audience.) Hey, look . . . isn't that Robert Redford?

A: (Assistant's eyes light up and she steps toward the audience to get a better look.) Where, where?

D: (As she is looking out into the audience Dropo stacks the boxes end-to-end by hand.) Well, there I did it. Didn't I tell you anything you could do I could easily do?

A: (Assistant has been holding boxes in an end-to-end balance the whole time.) OK, can you do this? (She now drops the boxes into a *side-to-side balance.*)

D: (Dropo looks flabbergasted.) Ah . . . why sure. (Hesitantly he tries this maneuver but drops all the boxes. They land on his toe and he yells in pain.) YOOOW! . . . I ah . . . I just slipped let me try it again.

A: (As Dropo bends down to pick up the boxes, his assistant accidentally lets the boxes she's holding slip and fall. She keeps hold of the bottom box but the other two dangle freely revealing the trick to the audience. She signals to the audience to be silent.) Shh!

D: (Dropo does not witness the mishap and proceeds to do the trick. Realizing he could never do it, he fakes it by catching the boxes in his arms and stacking them one at a time. Assistant shakes her head—no. Flustered he throws the boxes down.) Oh, the audience doesn't want to see this stuff, let's move on . . .

THE IMPOSSIBLE TRICK

Props: Three cigar boxes and one ball.

This is a nice little routine which requires no actual juggling or cigar box manipulations. Although this act has no juggling tricks, it makes a good finale to a juggling or cigar box routine.

"I shall now bewilder you with one of the hardest juggling tricks known to mankind. This trick was shown to me by an old Bohemian gypsy while I was traveling across Southern Europe. He was a very clever juggler and master of trickery and deceit. I paid him $500 to show me this trick. So, for the first time before a live audience I—Dr. Dropo—will perform for you the hardest juggling trick known to man. I will perform for you what is known as the Impossible Trick.

"Why, you might ask, is it called the Impossible Trick? Because it is virtually impossible to do. But I, the Great Dropo, will do it for you today. So what makes this trick so difficult? Let me describe it. I will toss these three cigar boxes and this ball high up into the air, and when they come down I will catch them in the palm of my hand one on top of the other in a perfect *end-to-end balance* with the ball balanced at the very top. But wait that's not all, to make the trick even more difficult I will do it with my eyes closed and while standing on one foot! Amazing you say—yes it is, but that is what you are about to witness.

The juggler holds the props in a ready position and looks over to his assistant. "Drum roll, please." His assistant honks a bicycle horn. HONK-HONK.

The juggler looks shocked. "What was that?"

"We didn't bring the drum today," his assistant explains, "and this is all I could find."

"Oh, all right" he says. "Drum roll, please."

HONK-HONK.

"Here I go—the Impossible Trick. The juggler closes his eyes, stands on one leg, and tosses the boxes and the ball over his head and behind his back where they drop to the floor. He reaches out his hands as if the boxes would fall into them, but nothing happens. He moves his hands a little as if to feel for them. One eye slowly opens and looks around, finding nothing. The other eye opens. He looks skyward as if the boxes and the ball were suspended above his head. He doesn't see anything, he looks left, then right. "Hay what happened? Where are they?"

Confused he looks on the ground and sees them on the floor behind his back. Embarrassed he says, "How did they get back there? Must have been a strong gust of wind. Let me try this again."

He picks them up, closes his eyes, lifts one foot up, and tosses them behind his back. Again they drop on the floor behind him. The great Dropo reaches out his hands to grab the falling props, but nothing happens. One eye pops open, then the other. He looks up again, placing his hands on his hips as if disgusted. Looking for them he turns his head from side to side. Hesitantly he looks behind him on the floor. Again he looks embarrassed and picks up the props to try a third time. "This is a very difficult trick. I must be putting too much swing in my arms for them to fall behind me. Let me try it again with less swing. I'm sure I'll get it this time."

He attempts it again. But this time the props go straight up and come down hitting him on the head. "Ouch ouch ouch!"

Rubbing his bruised head and looking exasperated he exclaims, "Well . . . what did you expect? I told you it was an impossible trick!"

DR. DROPO'S BALLOON SCULPTURING FOR BEGINNERS

by Bruce Fife

Rubber rabbits . . . bubbly bees . . . balloon dogs, camels, and kangaroos. These are just a few of the colorful rubbery animals that can be created out of simple balloons.

Used by clowns and magicians to delight and entertain audiences, the art of balloon sculpturing is now available to everyone. In this delightful book clown balloonologist, Dr. Dropo, shares his secrets for making several popular balloon animals, toys, and games.

Includes the following: giraffe, frog, mouse, swan, ladybug, squirrel, hummingbird, seal balancing a ball on his nose, Mr. Wrinkle, bubble baby, Captain Marvel, troll, Ziggy, Bubbles the clown, airplane, flyers, spinners, whistlers, fearless Freddy Fly Fighter, pirate sword, a balloon gun that shoots bubbly bullets, and many others.

Comes complete with a package of modeling balloons. All you need to add is the air. Price $5.50 postage paid.

Mail your order to Java Publishing Co., Dept C, P.O. Box 1564, Bellaire, Texas 77401

Send a long self-addressed stamped envelope for a free descriptive brochure of other books from Java Publishing Co.

CREATIVE CLOWNING

Edited and Compiled by Bruce Fife
Foreword by Richard Snowberg
President, World Clown Association

A delightful book on the art of being a funny clown. Contains 224 large pages (8.5" x 11") with over 200 illustrations.

Some of the topics include: comedy magic • balloon sculpturing • funny juggling • balancing buffoonery • fun with puppets • clown music • mime and physical comedy • stilt walking and unicycling • clown makeup and wardrobe • developing a lovable clown personality • controlling an audience • creative use of props • how to create jokes and funny routines • how to tell jokes and be a good comedian • how to start your own birthday party business • where and how to find good paying jobs as a clown.

Available at your local bookstore or magic dealer, or you can order it directly from the publisher (price $17.95 postage paid).

Send your order to Java Publishing Co., Dept C, P.O. Box 1564, Bellaire, Texas 77401